© 1978 Almark Publishing Co. Ltd.
Text © W. J. K. Davis
Colour Art & Linework © Almark Publishing Co. Ltd.

All rights reserved. No part of this publication may be reproduced, stored in a retrieval system or transmitted by any means electronic, mechanical, or by photocopying, without prior permission of the publishers.

First Published 1978.

ISBN 0 85524 296 5

Panzer Regiments.

By
W. J. K. Davies

Photographic Credits
SQUADRON SIGNAL ARCHIVE
IMPERIAL WAR MUSEUM
BUNDES ARCHIVE
APC ARCHIVE

Distributed in the U. S. A. by
Squadron/Signal Publications Inc.,
3461, East Ten Mile Road,
Warren, Michigan 48091.

Printed in Great Britain by
Edwin Snell Printers,
Babylon Hill, Yeovil,
Somerset,
for the publishers, Almark Publishing Co. Ltd.
49 Malden Way, New Malden,
Surrey KT3 6EA, England.

Almark Publishing Co. Ltd., London

Regimental commander's 'Panther' with infantry, who are armed with MP43's (later Stg43/44) an MG42 and 'Panzerfausts'. Note the variety of equipment and the uniforms worn by these troops.

INTRODUCTION

When, in the late 1920s and early 1930s, the Germans started secretly to rebuild their armed forces, various influences were instrumental in shaping them. In particular three things – the cavalry tradition; the desire to create an impressive 'showpiece' army; the new theories of armoured warfare being purveyed by the British expert Liddel Hart and others – combined to lead the General Staff to develop the concept of a lightning war of movement, the *Blitzkrieg.* This in turn emphasised a need for mobile, hard–hitting spearhead forces both to make an initial breakthrough and then to exploit it.

In the German army these forces were originally envisaged as of three types:

1. *The Panzer,* (or armoured), *Divisions* which would make the breakthrough.
2. *The Leichte,* (or light), *Divisions* which were to be the heirs of the reformed cavalry divisions exploiting the opportunities created by the *Panzers.*
3. Motorised infantry divisions which would consolidate the gains.

All would be highly mobile and the first two would incorporate an armoured element to act as the spearhead. Indeed originally the *Panzer Divisions* were to be almost entirely tank *(panzerkamfwagen)* divisions with only weak motorised artillery and infantry support. The Light Divisions were to have a great deal of light armour, their established 'cavalry' regiments hopefully being mounted on a new family of half-tracked carriers while an armoured unit of light tanks would provide speedy firepower.

Once Hitler came to power, this programme was implemented and development of the new weapons brought into the open. Unfortunately reality proved rather less grandiose than ideals, development and production of armoured vehicles in particular being slower than expected. As a result the intended five *Panzer Divisions* had to be formed with *'ersatz'* (substitute) equipment. Even dummy wooden tanks mounted on car chassis were pressed into service for training purposes and the tank units were equipped largely with the interim *Panzerkampfwagen I* and *II (Pzkpfw I and II).* The former was little more than a fast, lightly armoured machine gun carrier and the latter mounted only a light cannon but they looked impressive, provided excellent training and, in the early stages of the war, proved surprisingly effective against unprepared enemies.

The planned four light divisions, in consequence, were even more hampered. They were to have had an armoured battalion composed of a special *Pzkpfw II* reconnaissance variant but very few of these were produced and the efficient but complex half-tracked carriers were stillborn. Indeed up to 1939 these Divisions still retained mounted regiments as their main fighting component.

In that year, however, they were all hurriedly converted to fully fledged *Panzer Divisions* using whatever equipment could be scraped up and a further *Panzer Division,* the 10th, was also improvised for the Polish campaign of September 1939. Fortunately the equipment position had been slightly eased by the annexation of Czechoslovakia in March of that year, the German army suddenly acquiring thereby a collection of several hundred efficient modern tanks together with additional production facilities. In addition production of the standard *Pzkpfw III* and *IV* was slowly building up. On the other hand, the panzerisation of the light divisions meant that the follow-up forces were no longer there and early campaigns illustrated the danger of allowing pure tank forces to break through on their own. As a result, the *Panzer Divisions* themselves were reorganised with fewer tanks and more infantry while some motorized infantry formations were upgraded to what were known as *Panzer Grenadier,* (or armoured infantry), *Divisions.* These were strong, fully mobile formations with good support units and an armoured *Abteilung* (a battalion-sized unit) rather than a full armoured regiment. Since modern battle tanks were always in short supply the *Abteilung* was usually equipped either with assault guns or with outdated tanks modified for the close support role. This was not too great a handicap since the *Abteilungen* was intended mainly to provide the support which specialised infantry tanks gave in other armies. As the war progressed, too, additional armoured *Abteilungen* were formed outside divisions and used as army or corps troops. They were most commonly heavy tank units and in turn were sometimes incorporated into *Panzer* brigades which included battalion-sized infantry and artillery support units. The original ten *Panzer Divisions* were expanded to a total of 27 *Wehrmacht* and 7 *SS* formations before the war ended although their effectiveness varied greatly.

The *panzer* units to be described in this book were always the heart of the striking force and, so far as possible, those in the *SS* and certain crack army divisions were kept up to strength with standard vehicles. Panzer formations acting in a defensive role, or those on minor fronts, however, frequently had to make do with sub-standard equipment, assault guns instead of tanks or even captured enemy vehicles. Equipment issued to a division withdrawn for refitting depended on what was available at the time. It is impossible to cover all eventualities and the details that follow represent what was intended. It should be noted that even the planners recognised three categories: the *Grund Gliederung* or basic establishment which was the notional plan of what an ideal division should contain; the *Zoll Gliederung* or planned establishment which was what they thought they could provide for a particular divison when raised or refitted; and the *1st Gliederung* which showed what a division actually had at a particular point in time. Resemblance between

Pzkpfw Ausf. A's of the early wehrmacht fording a stream. The tank crews are not wearing Nazi insignia on their uniforms which came later with an order dated 30th October 1935.

Grund and *1st* might well be mainly coincidental!

To avoid continual repetition and explanation, standard German army terms and organisation symbols have been used throughout this book. The main differences in nomenclature are:

(1) The German tank or *Panzer Regiment* is a formation which equates roughly to the contemporary British brigade, being composed of two or more *Abteilungen.* An *Abteilung* is a unit roughly equivalent to a British or American battalion, possessing its own administrative headquarters and having two or more sub-units of company size. In German parlance such a unit, equivalent to a British tank squadron, was normally known as a *Kompanie* since cavalry terms were not common in the *Wehrmacht,* and its components were called *Zuge* (s. Zug). This is best translated as platoon. The headquarters was referred to as the *Stabs* (staff) and its administrative support unit was the *Stabskompanie.* Attached might also be such items as a support unit *(Versorgungs..),* an engineer platoon *(Pionier-zug)* a signals unit *(Nachrichtenzug)* and one or more supply columns *(Kolonne).* Units could be either armoured *(gegpanzerte,* or *gp);* motorised (mot.) or partly motorised *(T.mot).*

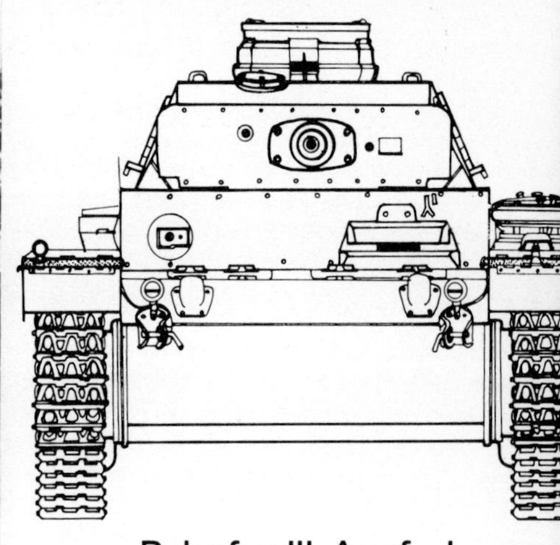

Pzkpfw III Ausf. J

Tank regiments were often in a position to carry their associated infantrymen on the march. Panzer Grendadiers boarding a 'Panther'.

A Pzkpfw III fording a stream to join the other vehicles of its regiment, Pzkpfw II's formed up on the other side.

(2) Equipment had standard ordnance designations: a battle tank was a *Panzerkampfwagen* (armoured battle vehicle), usually abbreviated to *Pzkpfw* with a type numeral after it. An assault gun, with its main armament in a fixed armoured housing, was a *Sturmgeschütz* (Stug.). An armoured personnel carrier was a *Schutzenpanzerwagen* or *Spw.* Most vehicle types had also an ordnance dsignation, either motor vehicle *(Kraftfahrzeug* or *Kfz)* or special motor vehicle *(SonderKraftfahrzeug* or *SdKfz)* with a type classification number that denoted its role. It should be noted that the type numbers for tanks (eg *Pzkpfw IV)* were not *mark* numbers as most British sources give them. These were indicated by the production variant code *(Ausführung,* or *Ausf.)* followed by a letter (eg. *Ausf. G).*

(3) Specific symbols were used to denote different organisations and weapons both on charts and on vehicles. These are described in detail in 'Wehrmacht Markings' 1939-45 'Almark' but some specifically associated with tank units are shown in Fig.1. It should be noted that all vehicles belonging to a particular unit carried its symbol no matter what their type (eg. a motorcycle belonging to a tank company carries the lozenge symbol). In addition all fighting vehicles carried a national marking, usually a cross, an individual identification sign and a divisional sign. Support vehicles had the divisional symbol and military registration numbers on normal numberplates.

PANZER REGIMENTS & ABTEILUNGEN WITHIN THE DIVISION

PANZER DIVISION HEADQUARTERS

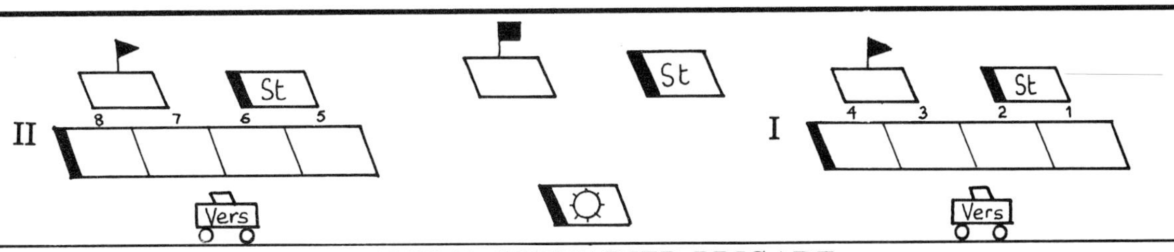

II 8 7 6 5 St Vers

St

I 4 3 2 1 St Vers

PANZER GRENADIER BRIGADE	
Regiment 2 (Motorised)	Regiment 1 (Armoured)
Anti-Tank Abteilung	Reconnaissance Abteilung
Artillery Regiment	

Ersatz Abteilung	Signals Abteilung	Engineer Abteilung
Divisional Services		

PANZER GRENADIER DIVISION HEADQUARTERS

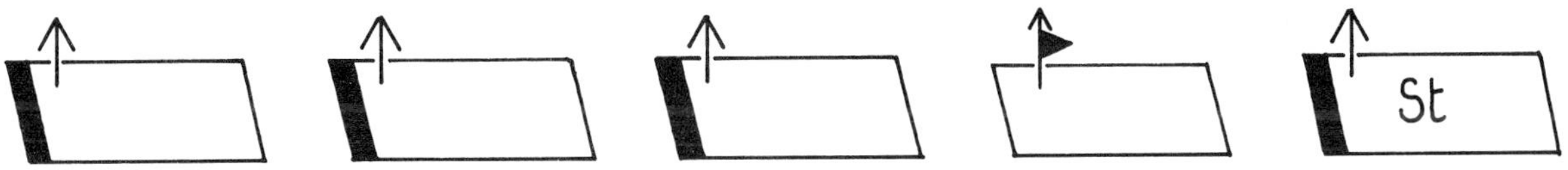

St

PANZER GRENADIER BRIGADE	
Regiment 2 (Motorised)	Regiment 1 (Motorised)
Anti-Tank Abteilung	Reconnaissance Abteilung
Artillery Regiment	

Ersatz Abteilung	Signals Abteilung	Engineer Abteilung
Divisional Services		

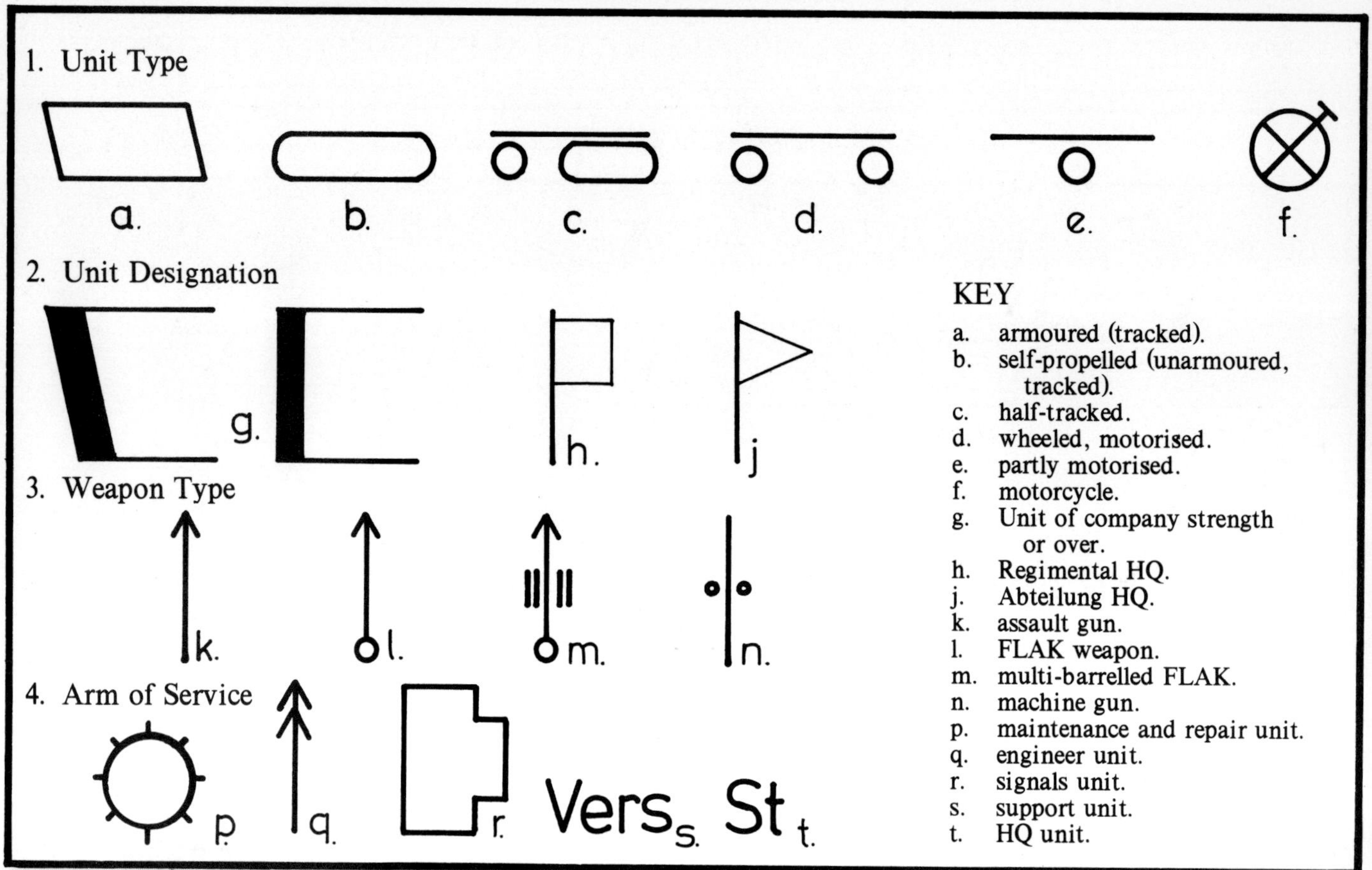

1. Unit Type

a. b. c. d. e. f.

2. Unit Designation

g. h. j

3. Weapon Type

k. l. m. n.

4. Arm of Service

p. q. r. Vers s. St t.

KEY

a. armoured (tracked).
b. self-propelled (unarmoured, tracked).
c. half-tracked.
d. wheeled, motorised.
e. partly motorised.
f. motorcycle.
g. Unit of company strength or over.
h. Regimental HQ.
j. Abteilung HQ.
k. assault gun.
l. FLAK weapon.
m. multi-barrelled FLAK.
n. machine gun.
p. maintenance and repair unit.
q. engineer unit.
r. signals unit.
s. support unit.
t. HQ unit.

LEFT: A Sdkfz 250 of the 24th Panzer Division leading Pzkpfw III's and Sdkfz 251's in Russia. The tactical marking on the 250 is for a motorised artillery unit.

Tactical Signs Particular to Panzer Units

Most of the signs and symbols used on armoured vehicles of the tank regiments were common to all arms of the German army. AFVs, however, had certain symbols peculiar to themselves which are described here for completeness. They were the means by which commanders in the field were able to identify individual vehicles within their command and consisted of a series of letters and ciphers painted on turret or superstructure. There were two basic groups, one for HQ vehicles and the other for tanks of the fighting companies.

1. HQ vehicles: Regimental HQ armoured vehicles bore a large **R** followed by a two-digit cipher indicating the occupant's job. Thus R01 was the regimental commander, R02 his adjutant and R03, normally, the signals officer. Tanks in the HQ company bore serials R04 onwards. Within each *Abteilung* a similar method was used but the ciphers were prefixed by large Roman numerals I, II or III as appropriate. It may be worth noting that this system only became fully operational after the 1940 French campaign; up to then some units simply painted on abbreviations (eg. Adj. for Adjutant) but this may have been because the need for clear tactical control had not been realised fully.

A regimental commander (left) confers with one of his subordinates. Note the HF aerial mounted on the commanders Sdkfz 251 half-track for long range communications to the companies within the regiment.

2. Company vehicles: Each tank or assault gun was allocated a three-digit cipher. The first figure indicated the company within the regiment (or in the case of an independent *Abteilung,* the company within the *Abteilung).* The second digit showed the platoon within that company and the third figure showed the individual vehicle within that platoon. Thus within a regiment there was no duplication and any tank could be quickly identified. A refinement of the system allocated special groups to command vehicles, X01 indicating the company commander and X02 his CSM, while platoon leaders took X11, X21, etc. With the *three-abteilung* organisation it was thus quite possible to have numbers in the 9XX range and these could also be seen in *two-abteilung* formations if a *Tiger* or assault-gun company was attacked.

Painting: Initially the signs were painted on detachable metal lozenges fitting in brackets on hull sides and rear. The intention was to make it easy to change symbols between vehicles as required but the small plates were not easily visible and sometimes became dislodged. From late 1940 onwards, therefore, signs were painted directly onto turret and superstructure. There were many variations some of which are shown in the illustrations. The plain white was often done hurriedly in the field and the variants with black or red outlined in white were more common. Red in particular showed up well against the later mottle camouflage and was often used where concealment was not an important factor. Signs were overpainted with new ones as required.

Crosses: The national cross in various forms was normally displayed on hull sides and rear. Plain white was used in Poland and the 1940 French campaign but thereafter black centred crosses were more usual.

ABOVE: A scene at a regimental headquarters in North Africa; a dispatch rider mounted on a BMW R12 combination is in front of the command vehicle, which appears to be converted single-decked bus.

LEFT: A regiment commander in his tank. His aid is wearing a reversible winter suit, plain-grey side outwards.

Regimental Headquarters Units

In considering tank units, most people envisage only the tank battalions but in fact both the regiment as a whole and each tank *Abteilung* had its own headquarters and headquarters company to control its operations. Furthermore, with the exception of certain specialised support elements, the headquarters organisations remained more or less constant throughout the war. Only the vehicle allocations and the numbers and types of fighting tanks attached to them varied.

Regimental Headquarters was divided into two parts. HQ itself consisted simply of three tanks, allocated to the regiment commander (R01), his adjutant (R02), and the regimental signals officer (R03) together with one or two dispatch riders. These tanks were in principle of the basic type forming the main armament of the regiment but equipped more lavishly with radio. In practice in the early days they were usually the *'Panzerbefehlswagen'* (armoured command vehicle) variant of the *Pzkpfw I, II,* or *III* which were true mobile command posts rather than fighting tanks and had no main armament; the later *Pzkpfw IV* and *Panther* variants were more commonly fighting tanks equipped with particularly comprehensive radio equipment.

To back up HQ, there was an HQ company *(Stabskompanie)* which provided fire support and administrative services. Its exact composition varied but it normally had four or five battle tanks (R04.. on) as a defence platoon, together with a motorised signals platoon and an administrative section with a few motor cycles or light cars and one or two armoured command vehicles based either on armoured car chassis or on the medium armoured personnel carrier *(Sdkfz 251).* These latter could, up to 1943-4 at least, normally be recognised by the massive frame radio aerials carried above their bodywork. The company organisation also included up to eight 3.7cm anti-aircraft guns. Initially towed, these were later, from about 1941-2, mounted on half-track or even fully tracked chassis so that they could manoeuvre with the tanks. Lastly, the company also had its own first-line maintenance and supply detachment – a rough equivalent of the British Light Aid Detachments (LAD) of the period. This included ammunition tenders and at least some unarmoured half-track vehicles of the 1 *tonne* and 5 *tonne* series since it was intended to manoeuvre with HQ.

From time to time HQ units were also strengthened by additional fighting vehicles. From 1941-on, as the *Pzkpfw II* was phased out of service with the tank *Abteilungen,* it was customary to attach a platoon of up to eight to Regiment HQ as reconnaissance tanks and this lasted until about the end of 1943. As the war progressed, too, troops of *Pzkpfw III* flamethrowers were occasionally attached for special duties. Six to ten was the official allocation but it was not always adhered to. *24 Panzer Division,* for example, had no less than 17 on strength at one period of its service on the Russian front and some British intelligence reports suggest that occasionally a few were allocated permanently to each *Abteilung.*

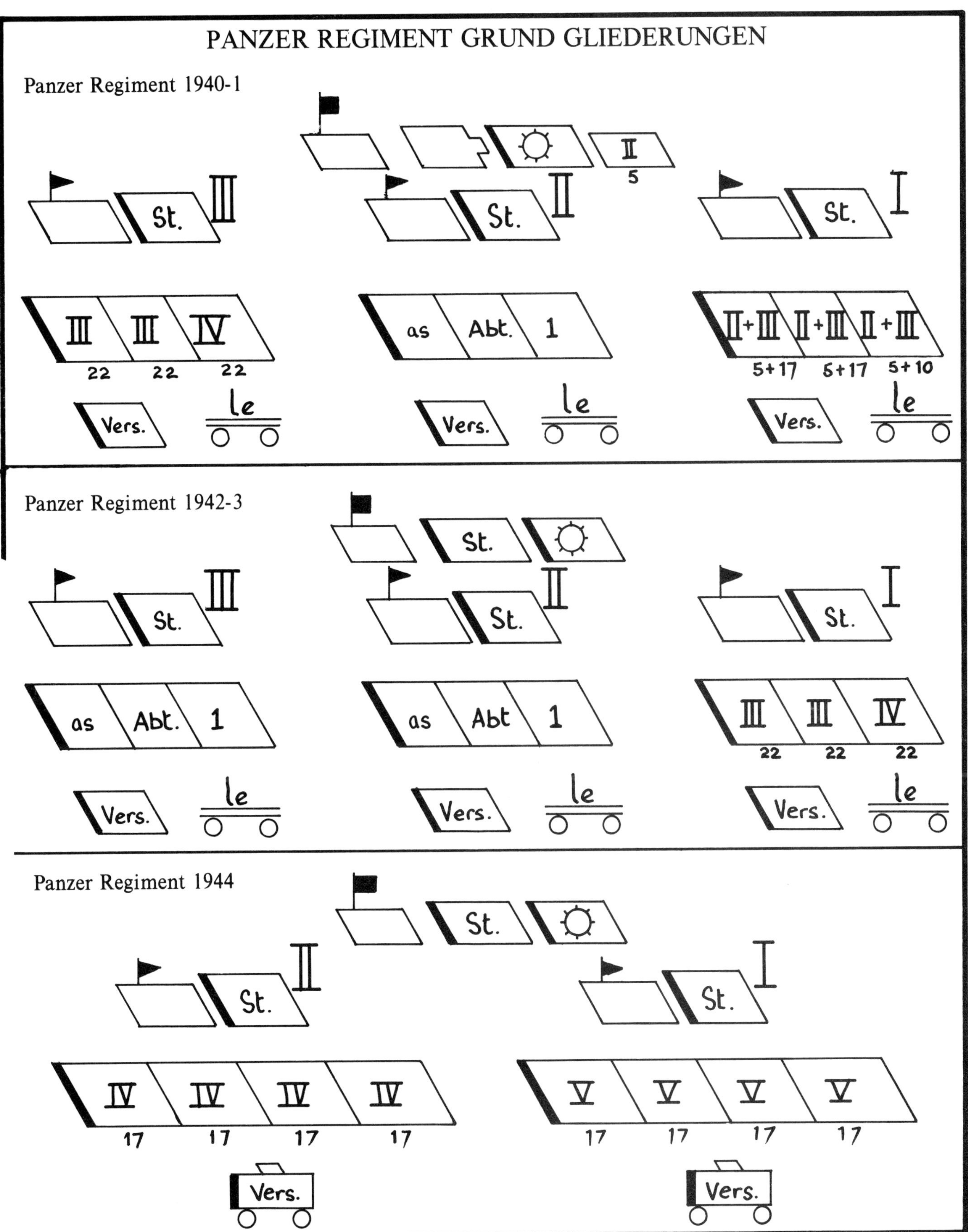
PANZER REGIMENT GRUND GLIEDERUNGEN
Panzer Regiment 1940-1
II
5
St.
III
St.
II
St.
I
III
III
IV
22
22
22
as
Abt.
1
II+III
II+III
II+III
5+17
5+17
5+10
Vers.
le
Vers.
le
Vers.
le
Panzer Regiment 1942-3
St.
St.
III
St.
II
St.
I
as
Abt.
1
as
Abt
1
III
III
IV
22
22
22
Vers.
le
Vers.
le
Vers.
le
Panzer Regiment 1944
St.
St.
II
St.
I
IV
IV
IV
IV
17
17
17
17
V
V
V
V
17
17
17
17
Vers.
Vers.

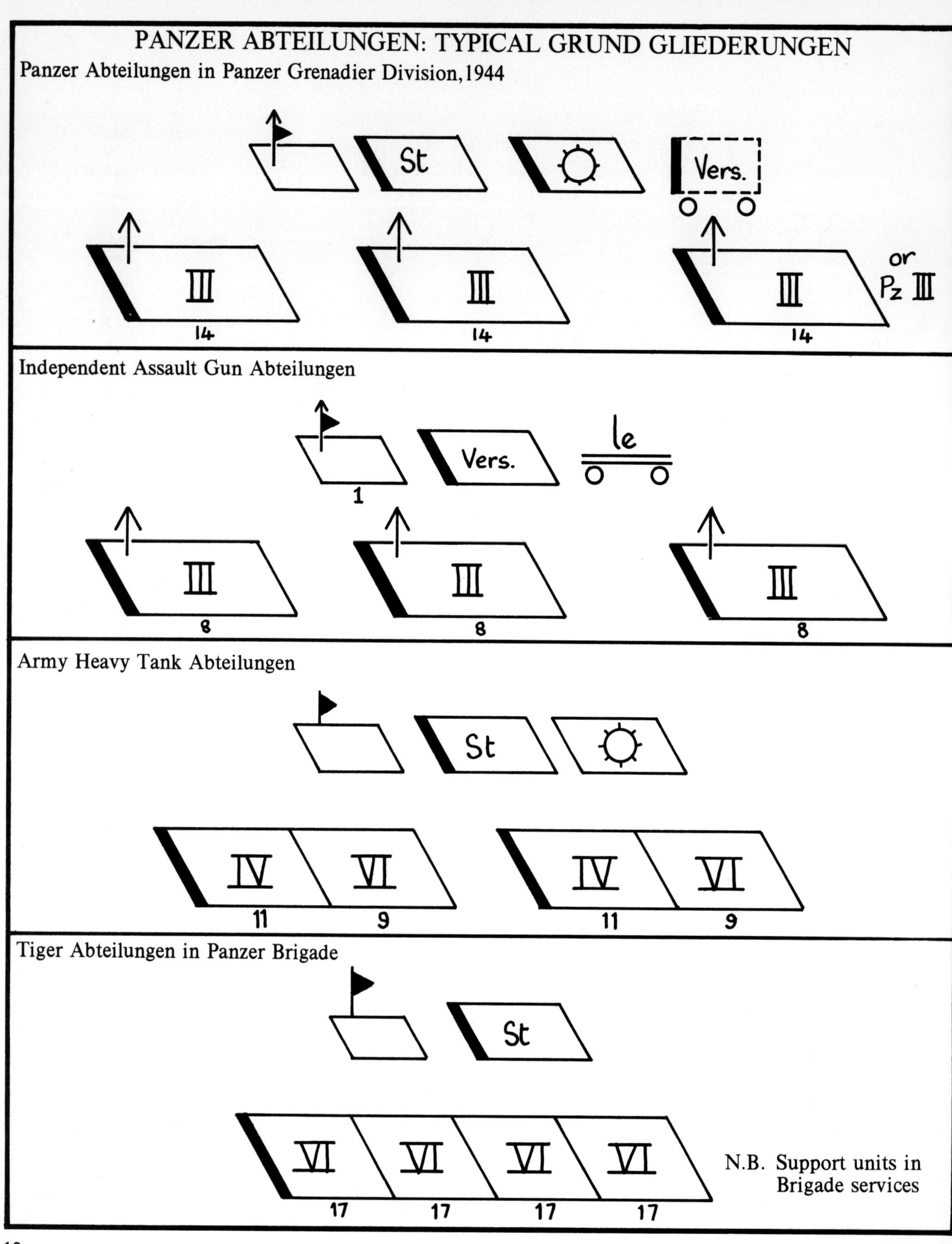

PANZER ABTEILUNGEN: TYPICAL GRUND GLIEDERUNGEN
Panzer Abteilungen in Panzer Grenadier Division, 1944
St
Vers.
III
14
III
14
III
14
or
Pz III
Independent Assault Gun Abteilungen
1
Vers.
le
III
8
III
8
III
8
Army Heavy Tank Abteilungen
St
IV
VI
11
9
IV
VI
11
9
Tiger Abteilungen in Panzer Brigade
St
VI
VI
VI
VI
17
17
17
17
N.B. Support units in
Brigade services

A battalion commander in conversation with two infantry motorcyclists, mounted on BMW R12 solo machines. The small command tank was built on the chassis of a Pzkpfw I Ausf. B. This example is fitted with an HF frame aerial in addition to the rear mounted whip. Note the MG34 in a ball mount for self defence.

The Tank Abteilungen

As can be seen from the organisation charts, the tank *Abteilungen* consisted of three or four distinct sub-units.

1. **Abteilung HQ.** This, like Regimental HQ, was theoretically divided into several parts. HQ proper consisted of three command tanks, although in later years at least these were more likely to be fighting vehicles than weaponless command posts. They were allocated to the *Abteilung* commander (01, prefixed by the *Abteilung* number in Roman numerals); his adjutant (02) and signals officer (03). In attendance was the HQ support company consisting of a defence platoon of five tanks similar to those of the *Abteilung's* main force (04 being allocated to the company commander); a platoon of 2cm anti-aircraft cannon; and a strong combat engineer and communications platoon. Up to about 1943 the latter were often a mixture of motor-cycle and lorry-borne troops while the AA component usually consisted of eight single-barrel weapons either towed or mounted on a half-tracked chassis. In the 1944 organisations, however, these were officially replaced by three self-propelled quadruple 2cm guns either on modified *Pzkpfw IV* chassis (intended equipment) or on semi-armoured half-tracks of the 8 *tonne* series so that they could operate with the tanks. About the same time the engineer detachment was equipped with five *Sdkfz 251* armoured carriers and assumed the local defence role. In addition up to about 1943-4 each *Abteilung* had a motorised-maintenance detachment and a light (60 *tonne*) motorised supply column. These were then amalgamated into divisional services but the engineer platoon was expanded to provide a first-line supply element. Total non-AFV strength was then fourteen lorries and cars, and eight motorcycles; it included a light command car for company HQ and three signals trucks, the remainder being largely stores and ammunition carriers. In practice these were a miscellaneous collection of whatever vehicles the bases could provide.

TYPICAL HQ UNITS

Panzer Regiment HQ 1940-2

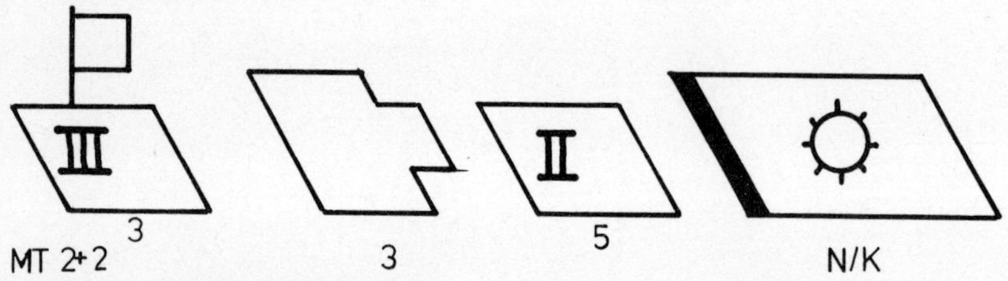

3
MT 2+2 3 5 N/K

Typical Strengths	HQ	COMPANY
Exact strength not known		

Panzer Regiment HQ 1943-5

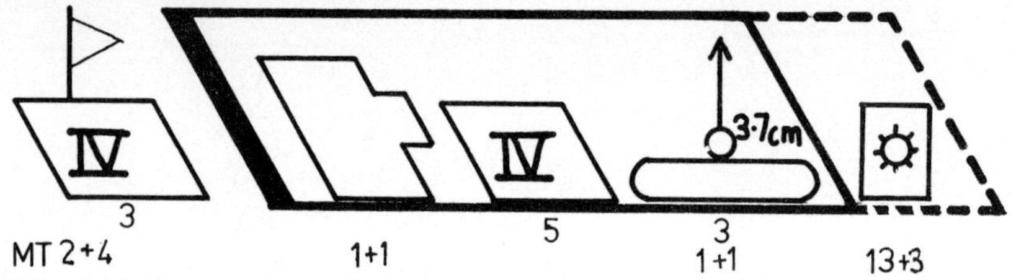

3.7cm
3
MT 2+4 1+1 5 3 1+1 13+3

Typical Strengths	HQ	COMPANY
OFF	4	4
NCO	3	51
ORs	7	54
MT	2 + 4	15 + 5
MGs	-	14

Tank Abteilungen HQ 1940-2

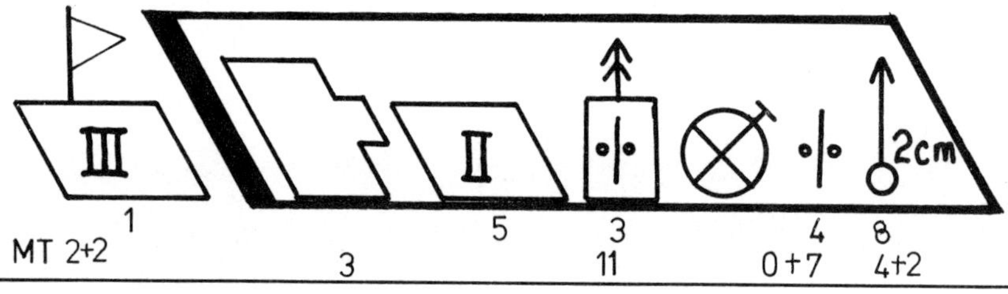

2cm
1
MT 2+2 3 5 3 11 4 0+7 8 4+2

Typical Strengths	HQ	COMPANY
OFF	4	4
NCO	3	32
ORs	7	99
MT	2 + 2	19 + 8
MGs	2	15

Tank Abteilungen HQ 1943-5

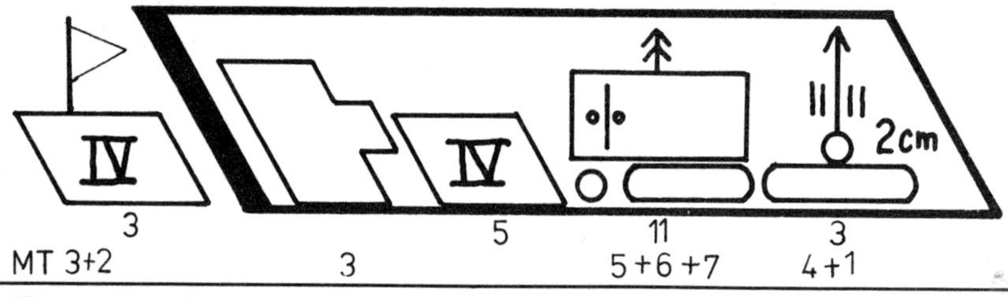

2cm
3
MT 3+2 3 5 11 5+6+7 3 4+1

Typical Strengths	HQ	COMPANY
OFF	4	4
NCO	3	32
ORs	7	99
MT	3 + 2	19* + 8
MGs	2	24

*Including 5 SPW

Tiger Abteilungen HQ

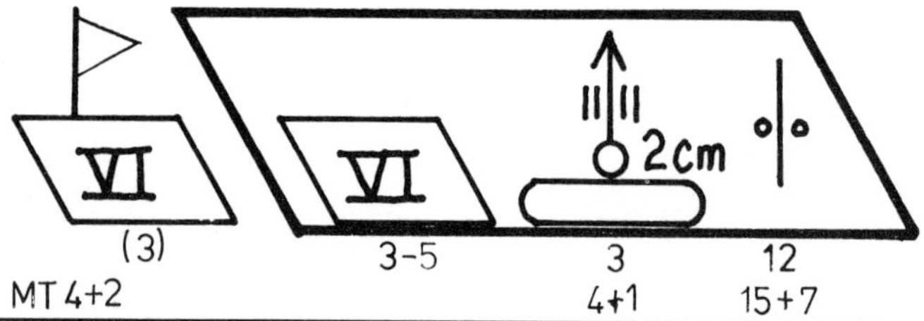

2cm
(3)
MT 4+2 3-5 3 4+1 12 15+7

Typical Strengths	HQ	COMPANY
OFF	4	4
NCO	4	27
ORs	7	89
MT	4 + 2	19 + 8
MGs	2	18

Army Tank Abteilungen

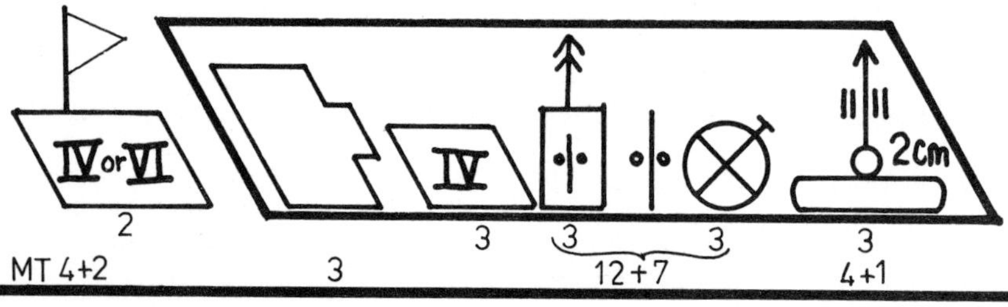

IV or VI
2cm
2
MT 4+2 3 3 3 3 12+7 3 4+1

Typical Strengths	HQ	COMPANY
OFF	4	4
NCO	4	27
ORs	7	89
MT	4 + 2	19 + 8
MGs	?	12

A Pzkpfw VI 'Tiger' in the process of being camouflaged by its crew on the edge of a wood. The Tiger was a heavy vehicle used by army tank companies and SS tank divisions. Its weight was its drawback and only 1350 examples of the Ausf E shown here were produced. Production was switched to the improved 'King' Tigers.

2. The Tank Companies. The varying organisation patterns can be read from the charts but these do not tell the whole story. Each company had its own headquarters platoon consisting of two fighting tanks with a support group of two light lorries or half-tracks and two motor-cycle combinations or *Kettenkrafträdern* (SdKfz 2). Total strength of HQ platoon, in 1944 at least, was 19 men and an officer. Then there were three (or in one 1944 organisation, four) fighting platoons of five battle tanks each. As originally envisaged in the 1940-1 scheme, these each comprised two platoons of *Pzkpfw III* or equivalent to act as battle tanks and one platoon of short-gunned *Pzkpfw IV* for infantry close-support work. In 1943-4, however, the *Panzer Grenadier* Regiments were allocated their own mobile close support weapons and so the organisation was changed to two, four-company *Abteilungen* each of a particular tank type. Initially the arrangement retained 17 tanks per company and although some 1944 organisation charts give a suggested company strength of 22 tanks this was applied only to a very few elite divisions on refitting. It would appear that *Abteilungen* using assault guns retained the normal organisational structure, the assault guns simply substituting directly for battle tanks.

It may be worth noting that in the 1943-4 period some divisions were strengthened by a heavy tank company of *Tigers* which was organised separately from the main *Abteilungen* and was regarded as the regimental 9th Company. Company organisation was normal and it came directly under Regimental HQ.

The armoured *Abteilung* of a *Panzer Grenadier Division* differed in some details since it had no regimental support. Thus it had a support company of regimental pattern in addition to its HQ company and in general the establishment was slightly lower. In particular HQ company had only three tanks or assault guns instead of five, while the tank companies, or more usually, assault gun companies had platoons of four instead of five AFVs.

Pzkpfw V Ausf. A 'Panther' (Sdkfz 171)

Equipment of the Tank Abteilungen

As described in the introduction, the original conception of the *Panzer Division* was somewhat delayed by slow development of its intended equipment. Consequently initial equipment consisted mainly of light armoured machine gun carriers, designated for propaganda purposes *Panzerkamfwagen I,* with an admixture of the slightly heavier *Pzkpfw II,* a 10 *tonne* vehicle mounting a 2cm cannon. These, it was recognised, were inadequate substitutes for the projected 'standard' *Pzkpfw III* and *IV* which were envisaged as a battle tank and an infantry support tank respectively, but they did provide the requisite numbers. They were supplemented from 1939-on by two efficient Czech tanks taken into service as the *Pzkpfw 35(t)* and *38(t)* which were simply substituted for *Pzkpfw III* in the establishment; and the comparatively small number of *Pz IV* required was achieved soon after war broke out. By late 1940, *Pz IV* companies were up to strength and *Pz III* were becoming available in quantity so, except in Africa, the *Pz I* was quickly phased out. By 1941-2 the standard establishment required three mixed *Abteilungen* of *Pzkpfw III* and *IV* though many divisions still had *Pzkpfw II* or *38(t)* substituting for their *Pzkpfw III* companies. By mid 1942, indeed, experience in both Africa and Russia had shown that even the 5cm gun of the upgunned *Pzkpfw III* was inadequate and from 1943-onwards the intended equipment was an improved *Pzkpfw IV* and the *Pzkpfw V* or *Panther ;* both were armed with long 7.5cm guns and production of the *Pzkpfw IV* had to be stepped up drastically.

The position was officially regularised in April 1944 by the promulgation of a new establishment based on a *Pzkpfw IV Abteilung* and a *Panther Abteilung* but losses always exceeded production and only a few refitted divisions ever received their full complement. A few divisions, usually *SS* or those without *Panthers,* were temporarily allotted a company of *Tiger* heavy tanks but many were lucky even to have a full *Pzkpfw IV Abteilung.* Their second one, instead of *Panthers,* was often equipped with long-barrelled assault guns which were effective in defence, better armoured than the equivalent tank and could be produced quickly. On quieter fronts new or rebuilt divisions in 1944 might even have to make do with a miscellany of captured vehicles. *21 Panzer Division* when opposing the Normandy landings, is stated to have included ex-French tanks and even on active service in Russia, hard-worked formations were often much depleted. *24 Panzer Division* for example, at a crucial moment in its career during the Stalingrad campaign, was hardly more than a strong *Panzer Grenadier Division.* Its 'established' *Panther Abteilung* was non-existent and its *Pzkpfw IV Abteilung,* in only three companies of 17 was composed partly of tanks and partly of assault guns.

The following pages describe in detail vehicles issued to tank units but do not consider variants used for other purposes.

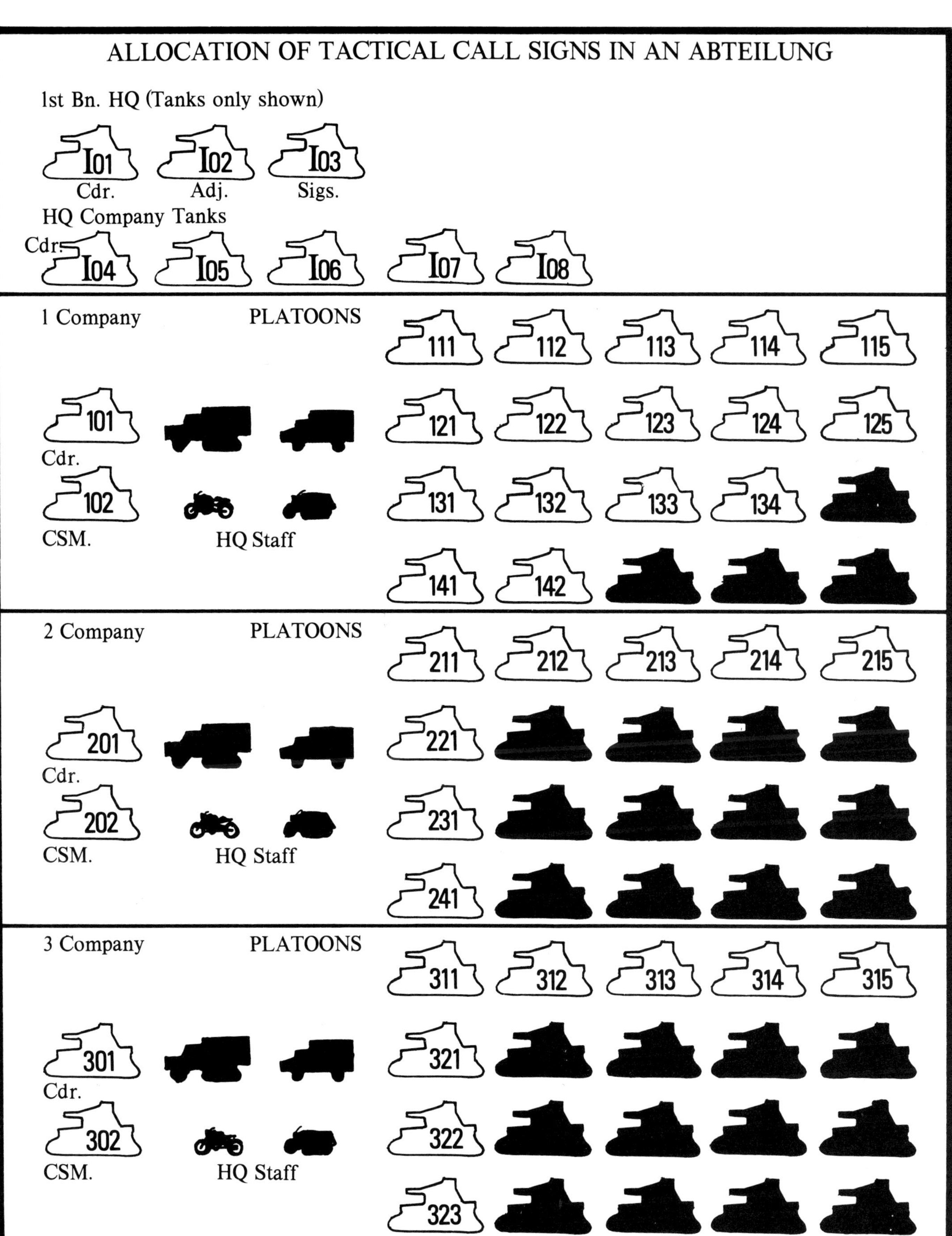
ALLOCATION OF TACTICAL CALL SIGNS IN AN ABTEILUNG
1st Bn. HQ (Tanks only shown)
I01
I02
I03
Cdr.
Adj.
Sigs.
HQ Company Tanks
Cdr.
I04
I05
I06
I07
I08
1 Company
PLATOONS
111
112
113
114
115
101
121
122
123
124
125
Cdr.
102
131
132
133
134
CSM.
HQ Staff
141
142
2 Company
PLATOONS
211
212
213
214
215
201
221
Cdr.
202
231
CSM.
HQ Staff
241
3 Company
PLATOONS
311
312
313
314
315
301
321
Cdr.
302
322
CSM.
HQ Staff
323

Panzerkampfwagen I and its Variants

ABOVE LEFT: Pzkpfw I Ausf. A (Sdkfz 101)

ABOVE RIGHT: Pzkpfw I Ausf. B (Sdkfz 101)

BELOW: Panzerbefehlswagen I (Sdkfz 265)

Pzkpfw I (MG) (Sdkfz 101) Ausf. A & B
Kleine Panzerbefehlswagen (Sdkfz 265)

The *Pzkpfw I* was the first tank to be taken into service with the *Wehrmacht.* Its design was started as early as 1932 under the misleading description *'Landwirtschaftlicher Schlepper'* – agricultural tractor – and in 1933 various firms were invited to submit prototypes.

The first accepted was a design by Krupp, using a Krupp, rear-mounted air-cooled flat-four petrol engine of 57hp with drive to front sprocket wheels and with a bogie-beam suspension using four road wheels a side. It had a two-man crew, the driver sitting on the left, and mounted two MG13, 7.92mm machine guns in a small revolving turret offset right of the centre line. Fighting weight was 5.4-*tonne* and 15mm thick armour was fitted all round. This vehicle was classed as *Ausführung A* and 150 were produced from 1934-on.

The more common variant, however, was the *Ausführung B* built by various firms between 1935 and 1938 to a total of 1500. The major difference was that it had a 6-cylinder 100hp Maybach water-cooled engine, necessitating a longer rear body and suspension unit with five road wheels each side. All-up weight was increased to 6 *tonnes.*

Both these variants were in service together on trials during the Spanish Civil War. They were really intended only to make a show and to provide training and experience for the *Panzer* troops; indeed some had open bodywork without armament and were used specifically for driver training purposes. Unfortunately, delays in standard tank production meant that they had to be retained in service during the first two years of the war, substituting in the regiments for *Pzkpfw IIs* while the latter substituted for *Pzkpfw IIIs!* No less than 1445 were on charge at the start of the Polish campaign and 543 were still allocated to divisions during the French campaign of 1940. Obsolete by then and surviving mainly because of the surprise and lack of effective armoured opposition, they were withdrawn or relegated to quiet areas as fast as possible. Some did serve in the early stages of the African and Balkan campaigns but they were effectively out of service by the end of 1941.

The only other variant used by the *Panzer Regiments* was the *Kleine Panzerbefehlswagen (Sdkfz 265)* of which some 200 were built on both A and B type chassis. This had an armoured fighting compartment replacing the turret, carried a crew of three with an armament of one forward-firing MG 13, and had comprehensive radio equipment for its period *(Fu 2 and Fu 6).* 96 were used during the French campaign by regimental and *Abteilung HQ* units but they were not very popular and were withdrawn soon after. Surplus chassis were used for various SP equipments by other units within the Panzer Divisions.

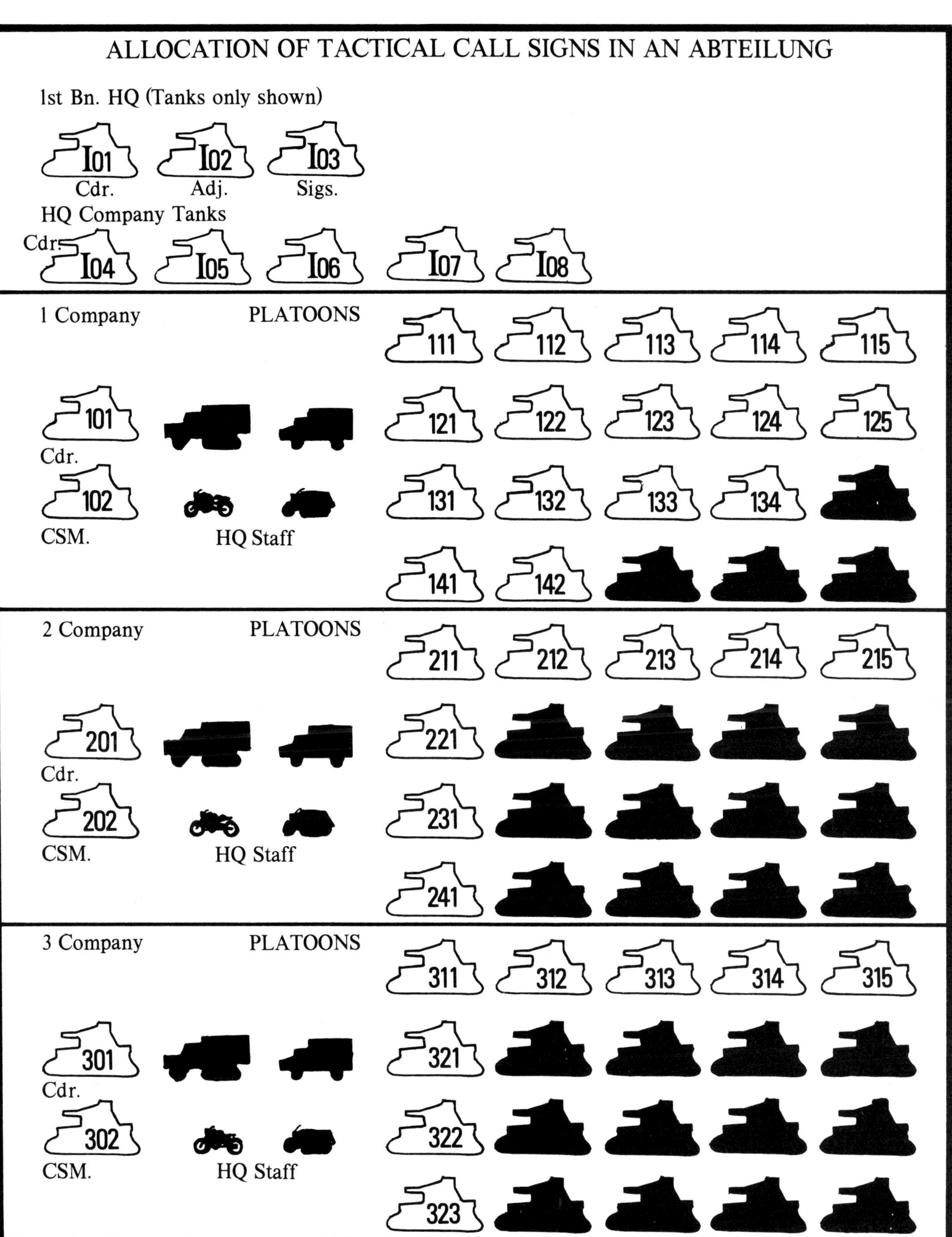
ALLOCATION OF TACTICAL CALL SIGNS IN AN ABTEILUNG
1st Bn. HQ (Tanks only shown)
I01
Cdr.
I02
Adj.
I03
Sigs.
HQ Company Tanks
Cdr.
I04
I05
I06
I07
I08
1 Company
PLATOONS
111
112
113
114
115
101
Cdr.
121
122
123
124
125
102
CSM.
HQ Staff
131
132
133
134
141
142
2 Company
PLATOONS
211
212
213
214
215
201
Cdr.
221
202
CSM.
HQ Staff
231
241
3 Company
PLATOONS
311
312
313
314
315
301
Cdr.
321
302
CSM.
HQ Staff
322
323

Panzerkampfwagen I and its Variants

Pzkpfw I (MG) (Sdkfz 101) Ausf. A & B
Kleine Panzerbefehlswagen (Sdkfz 265)

The *Pzkpfw I* was the first tank to be taken into service with the *Wehrmacht.* Its design was started as early as 1932 under the misleading description *'Landwirtschaftlicher Schlepper'* – agricultural tractor – and in 1933 various firms were invited to submit prototypes.

The first accepted was a design by Krupp, using a Krupp, rear-mounted air-cooled flat-four petrol engine of 57hp with drive to front sprocket wheels and with a bogie-beam suspension using four road wheels a side. It had a two-man crew, the driver sitting on the left, and mounted two MG13, 7.92mm machine guns in a small revolving turret offset right of the centre line. Fighting weight was 5.4-*tonne* and 15mm thick armour was fitted all round. This vehicle was classed as *Ausführung A* and 150 were produced from 1934-on.

The more common variant, however, was the *Ausführung B* built by various firms between 1935 and 1938 to a total of 1500. The major difference was that it had a 6-cylinder 100hp Maybach water-cooled engine, necessitating a longer rear body and suspension unit with five road wheels each side. All-up weight was increased to 6 *tonnes.*

Both these variants were in service together on trials during the Spanish Civil War. They were really intended only to make a show and to provide training and experience for the *Panzer* troops; indeed some had open bodywork without armament and were used specifically for driver training purposes. Unfortunately, delays in standard tank production meant that they had to be retained in service during the first two years of the war, substituting in the regiments for *Pzkpfw IIs* while the latter substituted for *Pzkpfw IIIs!* No less than 1445 were on charge at the start of the Polish campaign and 543 were still allocated to divisions during the French campaign of 1940. Obsolete by then and surviving mainly because of the surprise and lack of effective armoured opposition, they were withdrawn or relegated to quiet areas as fast as possible. Some did serve in the early stages of the African and Balkan campaigns but they were effectively out of service by the end of 1941.

ABOVE LEFT: Pzkpfw I Ausf. A (Sdkfz 101)

ABOVE RIGHT: Pzkpfw I Ausf. B (Sdkfz 101)

BELOW: Panzerbefehlswagen I (Sdkfz 265)

The only other variant used by the *Panzer Regiments* was the *Kleine Panzerbefehlswagen (Sdkfz 265)* of which some 200 were built on both A and B type chassis. This had an armoured fighting compartment replacing the turret, carried a crew of three with an armament of one forward-firing MG 13, and had comprehensive radio equipment for its period *(Fu 2 and Fu 6).* 96 were used during the French campaign by regimental and *Abteilung HQ* units but they were not very popular and were withdrawn soon after. Surplus chassis were used for various SP equipments by other units within the Panzer Divisions.

a
b
c
KENNETH M JONES 77

Panzerkampfwagen II and its Variants

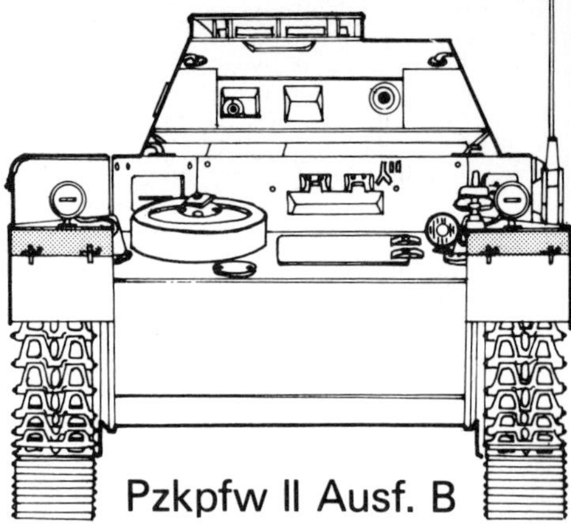

LEFT: Pzkpfw II Ausf. B (Sdkfz 121) with infantry. Note the commander's cupola, spare roadwheels and track stowage.

BELOW LEFT: Pzkpfw II Ausf. A (Sdkfz 121)

Pzkpfw II (2cm) (Sdkfz 121) Ausf. a1, a2, a3, b, c.
Pzkpfw II (2cm) (Sdkfz 121) Ausf. A, B, C, D, F, G, J.
Pzkpfw II (2cm) (Sdkfz 121) Ausf. D,E.

By 1934 it had become clear that, owing to the delay in *Pzkpfw III* and *IV* design, an interim battle tank would be necessary. In 1934, therefore, three firms were invited to build prototypes under the 'cover' designation *LaS 100;* the vehicle was to mount a 2cm cannon and one 7.92mm machine gun in a revolving turret.

Development was rather more complex than that of the *Pzkpfw I,* running through five experimental series before a definitive model appeared. The first batch, in service in 1935, was 25 examples of *Ausf. a1* weighing 7.2 *tonnes* with a rear mounted 6-cylinder Maybach petrol engine developing 130hp with a crew of three; *Ausf. a2,* the same year, accounted for another 25 with minor improvements to engine arrangements and in 1936, 50 vehicles of *Ausf. a3* followed with minor modifications. All three variants had 6 road wheels a side with suspension similar to that on the *Pzkpfw I* as did the 100 examples of *Ausf. b* which followed. The latter did, however, have an engine uprated to 140hp and the definitive tracks and drive mechanism while *Ausf. c* had the definitive running gear with five large, independently sprung, wheels a side. All marks had a 2cm *Kwk* 30 and an MG 34 in a well sloped turret and had a complex curved nose plate to the hull. Armour was 14.5mm all round on the 'a' series but subsequent vehicles had frontal armour increased to 30mm.

The major definitive versions were *Ausf. A, B* and *C,* the major difference from *'c'* being provision of a simpler, angled front plate. Some 955 of these marks were allocated to the *Panzer Regiments,* especially those of divisions 1-5, for the French campaign and so great was the need for battle tanks that they continued in production until late 1941; a peak of 1067 was then in service although they were seriously outclassed as battle tanks even in Africa. A further derivative, *Ausf. F,* and its minor variants *Ausf. G* and *J,* was however, built from 1940 through to as late as 1944 for use as reconnaissance tanks with the regimental headquarters units. It had strengthened armour (35mm front and 20mm elsewhere) which raised all-up weight to 9.5 *tonnes* and the G/J variants had a stores bin behind the turret.

The other main variants of *Pzkpfw II* used by the *Panzer Regiments* were the *Schwimmpanzer II* and the *Ausf. D* and *E 'Schnellkampfwagen'.* 52 *Pzkpfw II* of *Ausf. A, B* and *C* were converted to amphibious vehicles in September 1940 for use in the projected invasion of Britain, and allocated to the so-called *Abteilung A* composed of volunteers from *Panzer Regiment 2.* They were waterproofed, fitted with jettisonable flotation pontoons at track-guard level and equipped with a three-bladed propellor driven by extension shafting. Speed in calm water was about 10 kph and tests showed them to be reasonably safe in Force 4 sea conditions. They were never used for their intended purpose and were apparently reconverted to normal tanks soon after the invasion was called off.

The so-called *Schnellkampfwagen, Ausf. D* and *E,* were markedly different. They were intended as fast tanks for the light divisions and had a new, Christie type suspension with four large road wheels a side and no return rollers. All-up weight was increased to 10 *tonnes* and top road speed was 55 kph as against the 40 kph of standard models; superstructure was standard. 250 were built in 1938-9 but once the decision was made to convert the light divisions into *Panzer* formations they lost their intended role. Reading between the lines, they were somewhat delicate and non-standard, so their armament was requisitioned for new production tanks and the chassis were converted for various SP roles. The only one which may have seen limited service with the *Panzer Regiments* was the *Pzkpfw II (Flam) (Sdkfz 122),* 100 being converted to this flamethrower variant by 1940. A low open-topped 'turret' equipped with an MG 34 replaced the normal one and two flame projectors, each with a 180° arc of fire, were mounted on the front glacis plate. They could fire approximately 80 bursts of 2-3 seconds duration and had a range of only 35 metres. Most of these vehicles are known to have gone to special armoured units outside the normal regimental structure.

Regimental Commander's Pzkpfw II Ausf. B

BELOW: The Pzkpfw II chassis was used to mount high velocity anti-tank guns. The Marder II (Sdkfz 131) is shown.

Panzerkampfwagen 35(t) and 38(t)

Pzkpfw 35(t) (3.7cm)
Pzkpfw 38(t) (3.7cm)
The two other early types taken into regular service with the German army in 1939 were those acquired as a result of the annexation of Czechoslovakia in March of that year. The Czech armament industry, based mainly on the firms of Skoda and Ceskomoravska-Kolben-Danek, was then one of the most advanced in Europe and producing two excellent vehicles:

LT35 (Lehky Tank or Light Tank 35). This was a 10.5 *tonne* vehicle developed by Skoda and introduced in 1935. Around 200 examples had been produced by 1939 and most were impressed into *Wehrmacht* service, being allocated initially to the newly formed *6th Panzer Division* in lieu of *Pzkpfw IIIs;* it had 106 on strength at the beginning of the French campaign according to German orders of battle. Others were allocated to various allies – the Roumanians, Hungarians and Italians all had a few later – and at the end of 1941 167 were still on charge though then considered obsolete. Most remaining examples were thereafter converted to munitions carriers or heavy tractors and some may have served Panzer support companies in this role.

The *Pzkpfw 35(t),* as it was known in German service, was a simple rugged machine with rivetted armour 25mm thick at the front and 16mm at the sides. It was powered by a 120hp 4-cylinder, rear-mounted petrol engine, had a four-man crew and an armament of one 3.7cm gun (Skoda A3) and one 7.92mm machine gun mounted coaxially, in a revolving turret. A second 7.92mm machine gun was fitted in the hull front on a gimbal mount. The tank was not very popular with *6th Panzer Division* owing to its high silhouette but served competently until replaced by *Pzkpfw IIIs.*

RIGHT: Pzkpfw 35(t) and Pzkpfw II

BELOW: Pzkpfw 35(t)

LT38 (TNHP-S). This vehicle was the only foreign tank to be given the accolade of adoption as a standard type by the German ordnance department and retained in production. It was a 9.725 *tonne* machine designed by CKD at Prague and brought into use by the Czech army in 1938 – hence the designation. For its period it was an excellent fighting tank, fast but robust and mounting the 3.7cm gun and two machine guns then common. The armour was still rivetted but was ballistically well shaped. A rear-mounted 125hp 6-cylinder petrol engine, later uprated to 150hp, gave rather cramped room for a four-man crew; the sophisticated suspension with four large wheels a side mounted in pairs on beams gave them a reasonable ride.

ABOVE: Jagdpanzer 38 'Hetzer' on Pzkpfw 38(t) chassis.

The 200-odd examples in service were promptly impressed and production was stepped up. The 228 examples available in May 1940 were issued to *7th* and *8th Panzer Divisions* in lieu of Type IIIs and proved so useful that the tank continued in production until early 1942; at its peak, late in 1941, some 1095 vehicles were in use with various divisions, mainly in Russia. By 1942, however, the *Pzkpfw 38(t)* was outclassed by the Russian T34 and, since the turret ring did not allow larger calibre guns to be fitted, was gradually withdrawn from service or retired to less exacting fronts. The basic chassis was so highly thought of that it remained in production for various other purposes for the rest of the war but only one variant served with the *Panzer Abteilungen.* This was a 2cm AA gun mounted on the *38(t)* chassis in an open fighting compartment and taken on charge as the *2cm FLAK 38 L/55 auf Sf 38(t) (Sdkfz 140).* Some 167 were produced during 1943/4 for use by the *Abteilung AA* detachments. It had a 5-man crew, weighed 9.8 *tonnes* and was powered by the 150hp engine moved forward in the chassis to make room for the, rather cramped, fighting compartment.

2cm Flakpanzer 38(t)

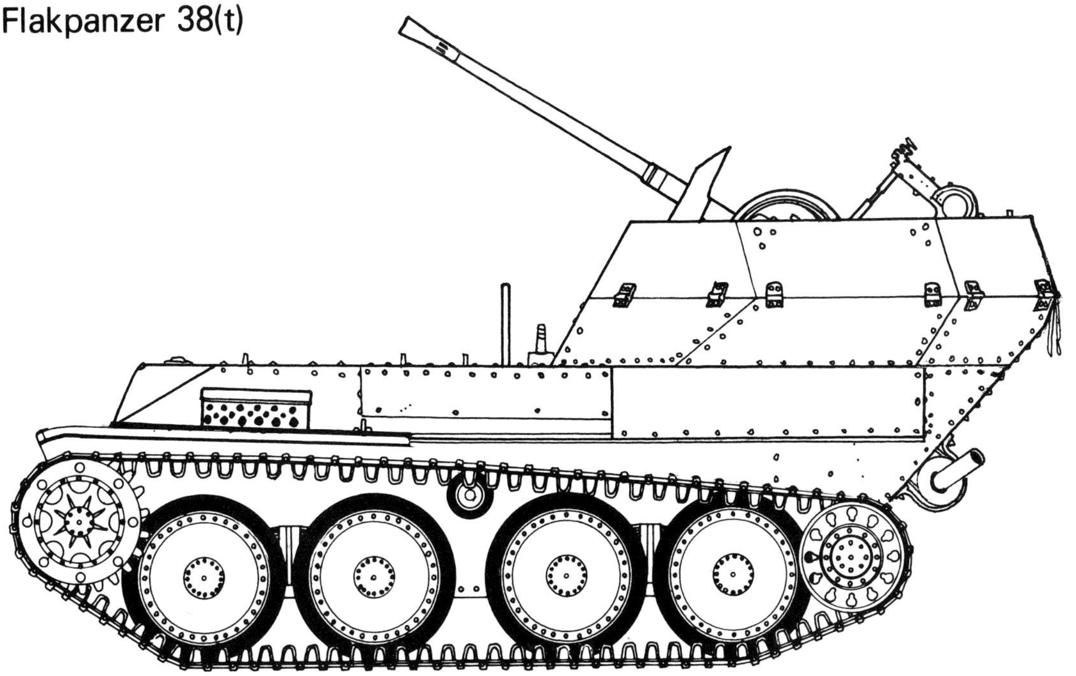

13

RIGHT: Pzkpfw III Ausf. J

TOP LEFT: Pzkpfw 38(t)'s

BOTTOM LEFT: Pzkpfw 38(t)'s with smoke-emitters on the rear exhaust.

Pzkpfw III (3.7cm KwK L/45) (Sdkfz 141) Ausf. A-D
Pzkpfw III (5cm KwK L/42) (Sdkfz 141) Ausf. E-H
Pzkpfw III (5cm KwK L/60) (Sdkfz 141) Ausf. J-M
Pzkpfw III (7.5cm KwK L/24) (Sdkfz 141/2) Ausf. N

Envisaged as the main battle-tank of the *Panzer Regiments* 'light companies', development of the *Pzkpfw III* began in 1935-6 under the cover designation of *Zugführerwagen'* or platoon commander's vehicle. Of all German tanks, the *Pzkpfw III* probably went through most experimental stages before reaching its final form. It was planned originally as a 15 *tonne* machine with a 3.7cm gun almost identical to the weapon then being developed as the army's main anti-tank gun and firing only solid armour-piercing shot. The prototypes, of which ten were built in 1936 as *Ausführung A,* conformed to the design, having the 3.7cm gun mounted in a slightly offset turret with two MG 34 machine guns and with a further MG 34 in the hull front. Engine was a 12-cylinder Maybach water-cooled petrol engine of 250hp and the running gear had five large wheels each side.

Ausführung B and *C,* 15 examples of each, followed in 1937, their main differences being in experiments with alternative suspension systems involving smaller road wheels, and they in turn were followed by 55 examples of *Ausf. D* at the end of 1938. These had an uprated motor of 320hp, 30mm armour all round with a consequent weight increase to 19 *tonnes,* and running gear comprising eight small road wheels in pairs on spring arms and three return rollers a side. As with other German tanks the engine was rear-mounted, driving front-mounted sprockets. All previous vehicles were reworked to this standard and in 1939 were issued to the original *Panzer Divisions* for trials, together with some examples of *Ausführung E.* This had the definitive running gear with only six road wheels a side and most had a modified turret with only one MG 34 mounted coaxially with the main armament. The vehicles were given war trials in Poland and some 349 are recorded as being available for the start of the 1940 French campaign, distributed mainly in the original five *Panzer Divisions.*

From 1940 to 1942-3 the *Pzkpfw III* was regarded as the main equipment of the so-called 'light companies' and went through a series of modifications to improve its effectiveness. As early as 1938, the fitting of a 5cm gun had been considered and the turret ring was made large enough to accommodate such a weapon. Early campaigns showed the 3.7cm gun to be inadequate and the 5cm *KwK* L/42 was installed in all tanks built after about mid 1940 as *Ausf. F.* This, besides the new gun, had an engine uprated to 300hp, a better cupola and a stores bin behind the turret. Only 96 were built before minor modifications produced the *Ausf. G* – which included some tropicalised variants – and the *Ausf. H* which had modified tracks and a simpler transmission; all-up weight was increased to 21.6 *tonnes.* Some 1924 were built with the 5cm KwK L/42 but in retrospect the choice was a misjudgement. It was unable to counter the Russian T34 effectively and from late 1941 a change was made to the more powerful 5cm *KwK* L/60, the tank then being known as the *Ausf. J (Sdkfz 141/1).* After the end of 1941 all *Pzkpfw III* brought in for major rebuilding were modified to this standard. It is worth noting, however, that over 300 vehicles with the 3.7cm gun were still in service in July 1941 and 131 in April 1942, presumably on the quieter fronts. The *Pzkpfw III* as a battle tank was already outclassed by then since the design did not allow of larger calibre tank guns being fitted but lack of anything better kept it in production through 1942. The *Ausf. L,* from the end of 1941, had increased armour, up to 70mm in places, and the *Ausf. M* had further minor modifications, continuing in small scale production into 1943.

The final version was, ironically, an adaptation of the basic tank to the close-support role. At the end of 1942 the *Ausf. N (Sdkfz 142/2)* was put into production as an infantry support tank for the *Panzer Abteilungen* of *Panzer Grenadier Divisions* mounting the original 7.5cm *KwK* L/24 gun of the early *Pzkpfw IV* complete in its turret. 660 were ordered but production was terminated in August 1943 in favour of assault guns on the same chassis.

4. Bergepanzerwagen III. Between 1939 and 1943 an unknown number of damaged battle tanks were rebuilt as recovery vehicles. They were stripped of their turrets, fitted with recovery gear and issued to tank maintenance and support companies.

5. Schlepper III. (carrier III). This was a stripped type III chassis converted for munitions carrying and used by some tank supply companies on the Russian front.

OPPOSITE PAGE TOP: Pzkpfw III Ausf. G's for the Afrika Korps.

OPPOSITE PAGE BOTTOM: Munitions Panzer III of regimental staff unit in Russia re-arming a Tiger with 88 mm ammunition.

BELOW RIGHT: Pzkpfw III's in North Africa. The top photograph shows a D.A.K. column on a desert road and the bottom picture a mixed column with motorcycles and Sdkfz 10 half-tracks towing 37 mm anti-tank guns.

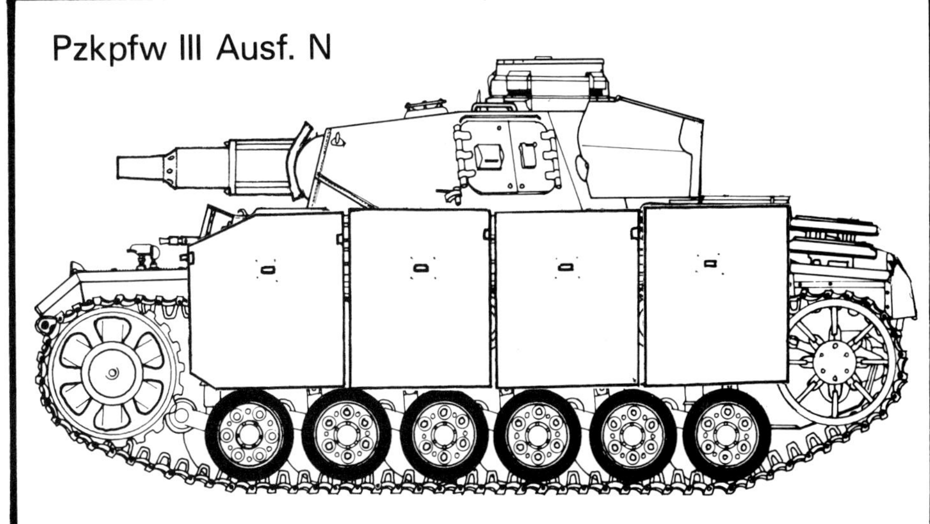

Certain modifications were fitted to vehicles of all marks from 1943-onwards, these being 5mm-thick armour skirtings shielding turrets and hull sides, and the batteries of small smoke-bomb projectors mounted on the turret sides. As a battle tank, however, *Pzkpfw III* was almost finished and from 1943 was in use mainly with units in quiet fronts such as Norway and the Balkans. In other roles several variants saw service with the tank units, however, and these are noted below.

1. Tauchpanzer III. In 1940 some 210 *Pzkpfw III* and *IV* were modified for deep wading and allocated to *Abteilungen B, C* and *D* of the special composite regiment established for the invasion of England. The work consisted of sealing all orifices and providing special ventilation and engine intake/exhaust trunking since the vehicles, unlike the *Schwimmpanzer II,* were expected to travel on the sea bed under their normal power. The vehicles were later allocated to *Panzer Regiment 18* for the Russian campaign and were used as wading tanks during the River Bug crossing.

2. Flammpanzer III (SdKfz 141/3). In 1941/2, 100 *Ausf. M* vehicles were fitted with a stubby flamethrower in place of the main armament. The equipment looked rather like a short 7.5cm gun, had a range of 55-60 metres and brought the all-up weight to 23 *tonnes;* crew was 3. The vehicles were issued to headquarters units.

3. Grosser Panzerbefehlswagen (SdKfz 266, 267, 268 depending on radio equipment). Three major variants of this command tank were produced from 1938-on, Nos. 1 and 2 on *Ausf. D* chassis and No. 3 on *Ausf. E* and *H* chassis (from 1940). They had a crew of five, a fixed turret and a wooden dummy gun replacing the main armament. Some 39 were in use with HQ units in May 1940 and 145 were in service at the end of the year. In 1941, a few examples of *Ausf. K* were constructed as *Panzerbefehlswagen* retaining the 5cm *KwK* L/42.

LEFT: Pzkpfw IV Ausf D of the 6th Panzer Division.

RIGHT UPPER: Pzkpfw IV Ausf J with an infantry machine gun section aboard.

BOTTOM LEFT: Pzkpfw IV Ausf C or D. Note the Mauser rifle slung on the turret rear. Rifles were not usually carried by tank men.

BOTTOM RIGHT: Pzkpfw IV Ausf. E with applique armour on the glacis.

Pzkpfw IV (7.5cm KwK L/24) (Sdkfz 161) Ausf. A-F1
Pzkpfw IV (7.5cm KwK L/43) (Sdkfz 161) Ausf. F2
Pzkpfw IV (7.5cm KwK L/48) (Sdkfz 161/1) Ausf. G
Pzkpfw IV (7.5cm KwK L/48) (Sdkfz 161/2) Ausf. H, J

The *Pzkpfw IV* was originally envisaged as the close-support tank to equip the 'medium companies' of the *Panzer Regiments* and was developed under the code-name of *Battailonsführer Wagen* (Battalion commander's vehicle). It should be noted that the tank was conceived as a parallel development to the *Pzkpfw III* and was designed as an 18 *tonne* vehicle powered by a 320hp engine and mounting a short 7.5cm gun. Krupp built prototypes and in 1936 their design was put into production as *Ausf. A*. *Ausf. A* was intended to be the definitive version, 750 being planned. From the start it had the definitive running gear with eight small road wheels, four return rollers and front drive from a rear-mounted 12-cylinder Maybach petrol engine developing 250hp instead of the planned 320hp. Hull armour was 14.5mm all round, weight 17.3 *tonnes* and armament one 7.5cm *KwK* L/24 with a coaxial MG 34 in the turret and a second MG 34 in the hull front. In practice only 35 were built and used for training, being replaced in production during 1938 by *Ausf. B* which had the hull machine gun mount suppressed. Its frontal armour was upgraded to 30mm, it had a fighting weight of 17.7 *tonnes* and an uprated motor. 42 were built in parallel with the very similar *Ausf. C* and equipped the medium companies of divisions engaged in Poland. During 1938/9 they were supplemented by *Ausf. D* and in 1939 by *Ausf. E* which was uparmoured to 40mm (hull) with 60mm frontal armour and a weight of 22 *tonnes*. It is interesting that, at that time, the *Pzkpfw IV* was envisaged as having only a subsidiary role and, once initial equipment was completed, production was sharply reduced, only enough being built to replace losses.

278 of all variants are recorded as available for the 1940 French campaign and an unspecified number (probably 52) was converted for deep wading to take part in the projected invasion of Britain. They were allocated to the heavy companies of composite *Abteilungen B, C* and *D* and went thence to *Panzer Regiment 18* for the invasion of Russia.

In 1941 appeared the *Ausf. F,* once more with strengthened frontal armour, better tracks and turret, and an increased weight of 22.3 *tonnes* but production was still slow. Only between 530 and 550 were in use during 1941. At the end of that year, however, it had become patently obvious that the *Pzkpfw III* was no longer adequate. The *Pzkpfw IV* was the only chassis immediately capable of taking a 7.5cm gun and so Hitler decreed it should become the main battle tank. *Ausf. F2,* produced late in 1941, was upgunned with the long 7.5cm *KwK* L/43 and used both in Russia and Africa as an interim version.

In 1942 appeared the 'definitive' battle tank, *Ausf. G (Sdkfz 161/1)* with 80mm frontal armour, a muzzle-brake for the higher velocity gun and, from August 1942, the very effective 7.5cm *KwK* L/48. Previous vehicles were retrofitted to this standard where possible and a total of 964 *Pzkpfw IV* was produced during the year. Early in 1943 there followed *Ausf. H (Sdkfz 161/2)* which had better rear armour and 5mm armour skirting plates, both on turret and on hull sides while in 1944 there followed *Ausf. J* with minor improvements; to save steel this mark was fitted with wire-mesh skirting since this was sufficient to detonate hollow-charge missiles.

In all a total of 8003 *Pzkpfw IV* battle tanks of all marks are recorded as being delivered before the war's end and the *Pzkpfw G, H* and *J* were the mainstay of the *Wehrmacht Panzer Divisions* right to the last. All *Panzer Regiments* from 1944 on were established for a *Pzkpfw IV Abteilung* and great efforts were made to ensure that this at least was kept up to strength so far as possible. Even up to 1945 the *Pzkpfw IV* was the equal of most allied tanks in the west and could give a reasonable account of itself against the T 34. Most importantly it was a reliable and rugged vehicle, a characteristic which went far to make up for other defects.

A variant also used by the *Panzer Regiments* was the *Panzerbefehlswagen IV,* produced for *Abteilung HQ* use mainly on *Ausf. H* chassis. This retained the normal armament but was fitted with comprehensive wireless equipment; the loader doubled as spare radio operator.

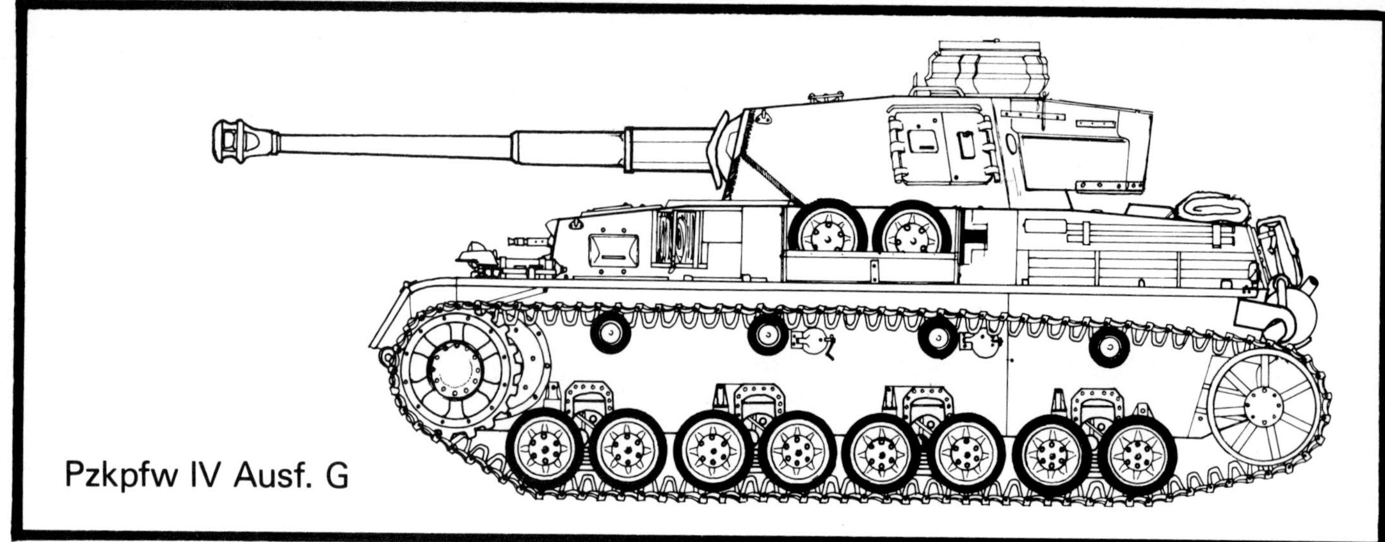
Pzkpfw IV Ausf. G

Panzerkampfwagen V 'Panther'

LEFT: Pzkpfw V Ausf. D 'Panther'. Note the early drum cupola, and two-piece hull side sponsons.

BELOW: Pzkpfw V Ausf G in sand and grey camouflage. This model has the one-piece hull sides.

BOTTOM: A knocked-out Pzkpfw V Ausf G. This tank has exhaust pipe guards fitted.

Pzkpfw V 'Panther' (7.5cm KwK42 L/70) (Sdkfz 171) Ausf. D, A.

Pzkpfw V 'Panther' (7.5cm KwK42 L/70) (Sdkfz 171) Ausf. G.

During the 1930s the design of a heavier tank than the *Pzkpfw IV* had been investigated from time to time but the design of the *Panther* stemmed directly from the first German engagements against the Russian T 34 tank in mid 1941. It was immediately realised that existing battle tanks were inadequate and Daimler Benz and M.A.N. *(Maschinenfabrik Augsburg-Nürnberg)* were asked to submit designs for a tank in the 35-*tonne* range to take a 7,5cm, L/70 gun then being developed by Rheinmetall-Borsig. Various prototypes were built, the M.A.N. design being selected although it was overweight (c 43 *tonnes)* and had teething troubles with both motor and transmission which were overloaded. A short pre-production run showed up these weaknesses and all subsequent vehicles were provided with strengthened transmission and an uprated Maybach petrol engine of 700hp. Production of the first major series, *Ausf. D,* commenced in November 1942 and the tanks were put into service on the Russian front almost immediately – with disastrous results. Engines burnt out, transmissions broke down, unreliability was such that more tanks were lost through defects than through enemy action.

Despite this unpromising beginning, however, the *Panther* turned out to tbe the best general-purpose tank produced by either side during the war. It was fast, mounted a powerful, accurate gun which was quite capable of destroying any enemy tank, and was well armoured. The armouring was ballistically well shaped, the hull being fitted with sloped armour to a maximum thickness of 80mm and the turret had sloped sides and rear with few projections. Torsion bar suspension was fitted and running gear comprised seven large overlapping road wheels a side without return rollers. As normal a rear engine drove front sprockets.

FAR LEFT: Pzkpfw IV Ausf D of an SS panzer regiment.

LEFT: The short 7.5 cm KwK main armament of a Pzkpfw IV.

The *Ausf. D,* of which comparatively few were built, differed from later marks in not having a hull machine gun mounting, merely a vision slit, and in having the commander's cupola built into the left side of the turret. *Ausf. A,* which replaced it in production during 1943, had some of the teething troubles corrected, had a hull MG 34 in a ball mount and a better cupola built into the turret top. It was fitted with 5mm skirt armour on hull sides only and was frequently issued covered with *zimmerit* anti-magnetic paste. 1768 in all of these two marks were built and their success was acknowledged by Hitler who made the *'Panther'* designation official in February 1944.

The final battle tank variant used by *Panzer Regiments* was the *Ausführung G* produced from 1944 onwards, to a total of 3,740. It had single-sloped armour and strengthened running gear. Like the others it had a five-man crew and was generally regarded as a very efficient fighting vehicle. The majority would appear to have been issued to the *Panzer Regiments* of *SS Divisions* and *Wehrmacht* formations in Russia although some were used in France, including those allocated to *Panzer Lehr Division.*

1. Panzerbefehlswagen Panther (SdKfz 267, 268). An unknown number of *Panthers* of *Ausf. G* and *A* were comprehensively equipped with wireless to act as headquarters tanks of the *Panther Abteilungen* and as Regimental HQ tanks. They retained their normal armament but can be recognised in photographs by the collection of vertical antennae sprouting from turret sides and rear.

2. Bergewagen Panther (SdKfz 179). One of the major problems in using heavy tanks was that the normal tank recovery procedures could not be used, since the standard 18 *tonne* half-tracked vehicles could not easily tow either *Panther* or *Tiger.* Consequently some 297 recovery vehicles on Panther chassis were built between 1943 and 1945,

ABOVE: The Bergepanzer 'Panther' (Sdkfz 179) recovery vehicle with a Panther tank in tow.

being issued to the tank recovery companies of those battalions having *Panthers* on strength. The basic vehicle was a fully armoured *Panther* hull with an open compartment replacing the turret. It was fitted with heavy winching gear, had a five-man crew and mounted a 2cm cannon for local defence. A few were stripped in the field and used as munitions carriers where conditions made supply difficult.

BELOW: The handsome Jagdpanzer V (Sdkfz 173) JagdPanther enabled the powerful 8.8 cm Pak 43/3 to be mounted onto the Panther tank chassis.

76 *tonnes,* on an extended and strengthened chassis. The hull and turret were better shaped, ballistically, and it mounted the 8.8cm *KwK43* L/71; there were two minor variants, about 70 having a Porsche designed turret built in anticipation of a contract and the remainder mounting the 'standard' Henschel turret.

A minor variant of the *Tiger I* was a recovery version which appears to have been improvised from battle tanks. The main armament was removed and the turret reversed, being fitted with winching gear. A few were used by *Abteilungen* using *Tigers.*

LEFT: Curious infantrymen around a Pzkpfw VI Ausf E (Sdkfz 181) 'Tiger'. The width of the combat tracks is noticeable in this view.

BELOW: Pzkpfw VI 'Tiger' in Russia. Although battle tracks are fitted the foremost roadwheel is not mounted on this tank.

BOTTOM: Pzkpfw VI Ausf B (Sdkfz 182) 'King Tiger' with a Henschel built turret.

Pzkpfw VI Tiger I (8.8cm KwK36 L/56) (Sdkfz 181) Ausf. E
Pzkpfw VI Tiger II (8.8cm KwK43 L/70) (Sdkfz 182) Ausf. B

The *Pzkpfw VI,* more commonly known as the *Tiger,* originated in 1937 plans for a heavy break-through tank but it first became 'real' in an order for a 45 *tonne* tank placed in May 1941. Henschel and Porsche competed, the Henschel design emerging as the winner and going into production as the *Ausf. H.* (This designation was officially changed to *Ausf. E* early in 1944).

The *Tiger I* was a heavy, squat tank with overlapping-wheel suspension and running gear and could be fitted either with wide tracks, for battle, or with narrow ones for transport; in the latter case, the outer set of the three sets of road wheels could be removed. It was a well-engineered vehicle with armour plating up to 100mm thick at the front and 80mm thick at the side; it mounted the 8.8cm *KwK36,* a modification of the 8cm AA gun with adapted breech and a muzzle brake, together with the usual coaxial and hull machine guns. Power was provided by a 650hp Maybach 12-cylinder petrol engine, later uprated to 700hp, and early versions had elaborate air cleaners and snorkel equipment for deep wading; it was realised that many bridges would be too weak to take its weight. This was eventually no less than 56 *tonnes* and caused some problems; it threw a strain on the transmission and made disabled tanks difficult to retrieve. The other main disadvantage was that the massive turret had a very slow traverse.

Nevertheless, the *Tiger 1* was an extremely formidable tank by the standards of its time. Only 1350 were produced in all, production being phased out in August 1944 in favour of the improved *Ausf. B.* It was normally used by army tank companies and *Abteilungen* but companies were attached to certain *Wehrmacht* tank regiments in Russia and *SS Divisions* had *Tiger's* in their establishment.

The *Tiger II* or *King Tiger (Ausf. B)* does not really concern us here since only 377 were put into service and it was used almost exclusively by independent companies and *Abteilungen.* It was an even heavier vehicle, grossing

Sturmgeschütz III and IV

Gepanzerte Selbstfahrlafette für Sturmgeschütz 7.5cm Sk 40 (Sdkfz 142)

Gepanzerte Selbstfahrlafette für Sturmgeschütz 7.5cm Sk 40 (Sdkfz 163)

The Sturmgeschütz, or assault gun, was originally designed as a close support weapon to accompany infantry attacks. The first variants *(Sdkfz 142 Ausf. A-E)* were basically *Pzkpfw III* hulls with the superstructure replaced by a closed, armoured fighting compartment housing a 7.5cm L/24 gun – known in this guise as a *Sturmkanone (Sk);* the gun had only very limited traverse. Weight was just over 20 *tonnes* and it had a crew of four.

These vehicles were tried out in 1940 and then issued to artillery units. In 1941, however, it was realised that, upgunned and uparmoured, the *Stug III* might form a temporary counter to the T 34 and, in early 1942, the *Ausf. F* was introduced. This had a 7.5cm *Sk40* L/43 as in the contemporary *Pzkpfw IV,* strengthened armour up to 80mm thick in places and an improved gun mount. From nr. 120 on, it was even further improved as *Ausf. G (Sdkfz 142/1)* by fitting the L/48 gun and in this form was frequently issued to *Panzer Abteilungen* of the Panzer Grenadier Divisions and also, as a substitute for battle tanks, to some *Panzer Regiments,* especially on the Russian front. Over 8000 were produced between 1943 and 1945.

The *Stug III* was supplemented in 1943-4 by an equivalent machine on the *Pzkpfw IV* chassis, the longer hull giving a slightly different profile. Otherwise the vehicles were very similar and the *Stug. IV* was used by several *Panzer Regiments* as a substitute for main battle tanks in 1944. Production was relatively small, being dropped in favour of the specialist *Jägdpanzer IV* early in 1944.

LEFT: Stug III Ausf G. This is an independent battalion commander's vehicle.

TOP RIGHT: Stug IV 7.5 cm Stuk 40 L/48 (Sdkfz 163)

BELOW: Stug III Ausf E in action.

BOTTOM: Stug III Ausf G late production model.

BOTTOM LEFT: A Jägdpanzer IV 7.5 cm Stuk 42 L/70 of the 116th Panzer Division.

Note on Captured Vehicles

As already mentioned, the German army adopted as standard equipment the Czech tanks LT35 and LT38 but this was not common practice; they happened to be available at the time when indigenous tank production could not cope with demand. During the course of the war, however, various other ex-enemy tanks were taken into German service and these notes describe those which came into fairly regular use. It should be noted that units of all armies often 'impressed' captured vehicles in the field if they were short of equipment temporarily but these were rarely taken on charge and were normally abandoned if they broke down. Besides such vehicles, two major sources of equipment became available to the Germans during the war.

1. After the French campaign of 1940, all surviving vehicles except those ceded to the Vichy government were naturally available. Most were either stored or converted to self-propelled chassis for various uses but four types were used in some quantity:

Char Moyen Renault R2. This was a medium infantry tank mounting a 4.7cm gun and one or two machine guns, with armour of 40mm maximum thickness. Powered by a

Pzkpfw 39-H 735(f) used by the Germans on 'quiet fronts'. Formally a Hotchkiss H39 of the French army.

150hp engine, it was already obsolescent by 1940 but was certainly used by some *Abteilungen* for local defence in France.

Renault B1 and B1 bis. This tank, the major French battle tank in 1940, was produced from 1935 onwards. It was a cumbersome-looking vehicle reminiscent of World War I designs, mounting a short 7.5cm gun in the hull front with a 4.7cm gun and two machine guns in a revolving turret. It was powered by a 6-cylinder 250hp petrol engine and had a maximum armour thickness of between 40 and 60mm depending on model. Later versions had an uprated engine of 300hp. Since a large quantity was captured, the type was used by the *Wehrmacht* for training *Abteilungen* and some may have been taken out of store for use on quiet fronts in 1944-5.

Somua S35. This was a good tank by 1940 standards, using heavy cast armour with a maximum thickness of 55mm and mounting the turret of the B1 bis. It was powered by a 190hp V8 engine and, unusually, had rear drive. It was certainly issued as standard equipment to German Panzer units, probably including 21st Panzer and 116 Panzer Division at one period.

2. After the Italian surrender in 1943, considerable quantities of Italian army equipment were taken over by the Germans. Mostly soft-skin vehicles were used but it appears that some *Carro Armato M13/40* medium tanks were issued to formations in the Balkans. The M13/40 was the standard Italian medium tank, rather similar in appearance to the *Pzkpfw 35(t)* and mounting a 4.7cm gun and an 8mm MG in a revolving turret. It had 30mm hull armour and 40mm turret armouring but was not a particularly effective fighting vehicle.

Germans examining abandoned French WW1 Renault light tanks. The wehrmacht used these as Pzkpfw 18-R 730(f).

Type	Ausf.	Dimensions								
		OVERALL LENGTH (m)	LENGTH OF HULL (m)	WIDTH OVERALL(m)	HEIGHT OVERALL (m)	ALL UP WEIGHT (tonnes)	MAX. ARMOUR (mm)	h.p.	MAX. SPEED (kph) Rd/X Country	MAX. RANGE (km)
Pzkpfw I	A	4.02	4.02	2.06	1.72	5.4	13	157	40[a]	145
Pzkpfw I	B	4.42	4.42	2.06	1.72	6.0	14.5	100	40	140
Pzkpfw II	D, E	4.64	4.64	2.30	2.02	10.0	30	140	55/19	200
Pzkpfw II (A, B, C similar)	F, G	4.81	4.81	2.28	2.02	9.5	35	140	40/19	200
Pzkpfw 35t	–	4.45	4.45	2.14	2.20	10.5	25	120	40	190
Pzkpfw 38t	–	4.90	4.90	2.06	2.37	9.725	25	125	42/15	230
Pzkpfw III	D	5.41	5.41	2.91	2.44	19.3	30	320	40	165
Pzkpfw III	E	5.41	5.41	2.91	2.44	19.5	30	300	40/18	175
Pzkpfw III	F-G	5.41	5.41	2.92	2.44	20.3	30	300	40/18	175
Pzkpfw III	H	5.52	5.52	2.95	2.50	21.6	30[a]	300	40/18	175
Pzkpfw III	J-N	6.41[b]	5.52	2.95	2.50	22.3	50	300	40/19	175
Pzkpfw IV	E	5.91	5.91	2.86	2.68	20.0	30	300	40/20	200
Pzkpfw IV	F[c]	5.93[c]	5.93	2.88	2.68	22.3[c]	50	300	40/16	200
Pzkpfw IV	G	6.63	5.91	2.88	2.68	23.6	50	300	40/16	200
Pzkpfw IV	H, J	7.02	5.89	3.29[d]	2.68	25.0	80	300	38/16	300
Pzkpfw V 'Panther'	A, G	8.86	6.88	3.43	2.95	44.8[e]	110	700	46/24	177
Pzkpfw V 'Panther'	D	8.86	6.88	3.43	2.95	43.0	80	650	46/24	169
Pzkpfw VI 'Tiger I'	E	8.24	6.20	3.73[f]	2.86	55.0[g]	100	700	38/20	100
Pzkpfw VI 'Tiger II'	B	10.26	7.26	3.75[f]	3.09	69.7[g]	150	700	38/17	110
Pzkpfw Stug. III	G	N/K	5.49	2.92	2.30	24.0	50	300	40/24	169

a road speed
b applies to versions with the L/60 gun
c F2 had overall 1. of 6,63m; auw of 23.6t
d width over skirt armour.
e Ausf A had auw of 45.5t
f width in battle order with wide tracks
g different sources give different weights, These are official figures but the more commonly accepted ones are those quoted in the text.

TANK DATA

Major Weapons of the Panzer Regiments

The 56 calibre 8.8 cm KwK36 of a Tiger Ausf. E.

ABOVE: The German 8.8 cm dual purpose weapon which inspired standardised larger calibre guns in tanks.

The heart of any armoured fighting vehicle is its armament and the Germans were fortunate in that, after the first year or so of the war, their main tank guns were always at least equal and usually superior to those of the allies. A gun can be considered as three major items:

1. The piece or ordnance itself, comprising the barrel and breech assembly with the appurtenances.
2. The sighting and ranging mechanisms.
3. The carriage or mount.

A tank gun is a specialised piece of ordnance, being of necessity a long-barrelled, high velocity equipment capable of penetrating targets at long ranges and with a very flat trajectory. The technical German term was *Kanone,* which may be translated as *gun,* as distinct from howitzers or other forms of artillery. German guns were usually described in terms of their calibre, year of origin and the calibre/length ratio of their barrels. Thus the 8.8cm *KwK36* L/56 was of 8.8cm calibre, originated in 1936 – as an AA gun – and had a calibre/length ratio of 56. In general one can say that the longer the barrel for a given calibre the greater was the accuracy and muzzle velocity but the more unwieldy the weapon became. It became common practice on the longer weapons to fit muzzle brakes *(mundungsbremse)* to help limit the recoil after firing.

In obtaining range, accuracy and penetrating power, the quality of the design is of course paramount and the German 5cm, 7.5cm and 8.8cm guns were certainly among the most advanced in the world for their period. They also had two useful features which were not always present in their opponents' weapons.

1. They were standardised: it was German practice to use the same design, with slight adaptations, in different mounts for different purposes. Thus the 7.5cm L/48 tank gun was very similar to the equivalent anti-tank equipment *(Panzer Abwehr Kanone 40* or *PAK 40)* and had an assault gun variant known as the *Sturm-Kanone 40.* The 8.8cm series was developed directly from an AA gun which had proved effective for anti-tank use.
2. They were deliberately designed as multi-role weapons able to fire high explosive and smoke shells as well as armour-piercing shot. This considerably increased their versatility in battle.

BELOW: The smallest German AFV gun, the 2 cm KWK here mounted in a Pzspw (6 rad) Sdkfz 231 heavy armoured car.

d
e
f
KENNETH M JONES 77

Allied to this innate good design were sighting mechanisms in most cases considerably superior to those of allied weapons, and in particular to those of contemporary Russian tanks. This gave the German crews a slight, and badly needed, edge over the Russian guns which were otherwise the equal of German equipment for most of the war.

The major types of tank gun used by the Germans are shown in Table 1. It will be seen that both calibre and length increased steadily, the limitations on each being the size and strength of the tank turrets currently available. They were all designed as anti-armour weapons with the exception of the 7.5cm *KwK* L/24. This was basically an infantry close-support weapon and was most useful when firing high explosive at 'soft' targets.

N.B. It is difficult to find accurate records of the penetrating power of tank guns. The table gives a general idea of the power of the more common weapons firing on single-thickness armour plate and penetrating at 90° (vertical to the line of flight) and inclined 30° from the vertical ('60°'). It has been compiled from Allied and German sources and it should be noted that most German sources give the rather odd ranges shown. These equate quite closely to 500, 1500 and 2500 yards and may be conversions.

Details of Major Guns — Table 1

Weapon	C/L ratio	M/V m/sec	Proj. Wt (kg.)	mm of theoretical armour penetration at:					
				457m		1373m		2285m	
				90°	60°	90°	60°	90°	60°
3.7cm KwK36	L/45	762	0.68	51	43	short range weapon			
5.0cm KwK38	L/60	823	2.25	78	47	61	40		
7.5cm KwK37	L/24	385	6.8		41	not really an anti-armour gun			
7.5cm KwK40	L/48	750	6.8	154	115	115	80	83	53
7.5cm KwK43	L/70	935	6.8	182	141		121		
8.8cm KwK36	L/56	810	9.4	130	110	109	94		
8.8cm KwK43	L/71	1000	10.16	207	182	174	153	145	127

ABOVE: Pzkpfw II's mounted the 2 cm KwK as their main offensive armament.

BELOW: Stug III taking on 7.5 cm ammunition. The rounds are handed up to the crew by 'human chain'. The size of the complete 7.5 cm round is clearly shown in this photograph.

Anti-Aircraft Guns

Integral in the *Panzer Regiments* and *Abteilungen* were also two major types of anti-aircraft gun *(Flugzeug-Abwehr-Kanone,* or *FLAK)* developed in parallel to their tank equivalents; there is, after all, considerable affinity between the two types since both require long range, accuracy and penetrating power. The light AA equipment was the 2cm *FLAK* 30, introduced in 1935 and supplemented in 1940 by the 2cm *FLAK* 38. They were good, reliable weapons with a high effective rate of fire (220 rpm) and even more lethal when mounted in a quadruple mount as the 2cm *Flakvierling* 38. Originally the single barrel version was mounted on its own two-wheeled trailer, towed either by a wheeled vehicle such as the Krupp L243 or by a light half-track, but later variants were often mounted on the 1-*tonne* series of half-tracked carriers (*Sdkfz 10*). The *Flakvierling* in regimental service

LEFT: Flakvierling 38 quad mount on a half-track belonging to a Luftwaffe unit serving with the 2nd Panzer Division.

BELOW: 3.7 cm Flak 36 on a half-track chassis. Note the winter reversible suits worn by the gun-crew.

was normally mounted on semi-armoured 5 *tonne* or 8 *tonne* half-tracked chassis although some were also built onto *Pzkpfw IV* chassis in 1944-5 as the so-called *Wirbelwind* (Whirlwind, with an open turret) or *Möbelwagen* (Furniture Van, with an open-topped fighting compartment).

The other equipment was the 3.7cm *FLAK* 36 and its successors the 3.7cm *FLAK* 37 and 43. This was the standard light AA gun of the German army and had an effective range of some 3500 metres as against the 2200 metres of the 2cm weapon. Like the latter it could be towed but in *Panzer Regiment* service was normally on a self-propelled mount. The 8 *tonne* half-track series was most common but variants on *Pzkpfw IV* chassis, *Ostwind* (turreted) and *Möbelwagen* (open compartment) were used in small quantities during the latter part of the war.

UPPER RIGHT: Flakpanzer IV 2 cm Möbelwagen

Anti-Aircraft Weapons — Table 2

Weapon	C/L ratio	M/V m/sec AP	M/V m/sec HE	Max Range in metres Ground	Max Range in metres Air	Wt of round in grammes	cyclic rate of (rpm)
2.0cm FLAK 30	L/55	830	900	4800	2200	115-148	280
2.0cm FLAK 38	L/55	830	900	4800	2200	115-148	480
3.7cm FLAK 36 3.7cm FLAK 37	L/60	770	820	6500	3500	623-658	160

RIGHT: Light 'flak'. A twin MG34 7.92 mm (Zwillings Lafette 34) mounting on a heavily camouflaged light truck.

BELOW: Elements of the 24th Panzer Division on the move. An 8 tonne Zgkw (Sdkfz 7) provides anti-aircraft cover with a twin 2 cm mounting.

2 cm Flak 38 mounted on a Sdkfz 10 'Demag' 1 ton half-track.

LEFT: MG13. This machine gun armed the early panzers. It is shown with its 75 round saddle and 20 round box magazines.

BELOW: MG42 being fired as a close defence weapon from a Stug III. This gun is an early production model.

Two main patterns of machine gun were used in AFVs of the *Panzer Regiments.*

MG 13K. This was a light, air-cooled, recoil-operated weapon dating from the 1914-18 war and sometimes known as the *Dreyse* gun, from the name of its designer. It had a cyclic rate of fire of 500-625 rounds a minute and the calibre was 7.92mm.

MG 34. This was the standard machine gun of the German army at 1939 and was the normal hull and turret machine gun for most indigenous tank types. It was a good, versatile weapon, air-cooled and of 7.92mm calibre with a cyclic rate of fire of c.900 rounds a minute and an accurate range of 6-800 metres. It was never replaced by the later MG 42 since tank mountings would not accept the latter.

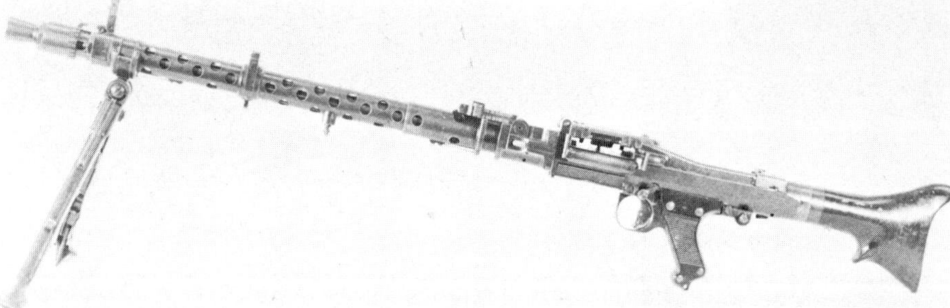

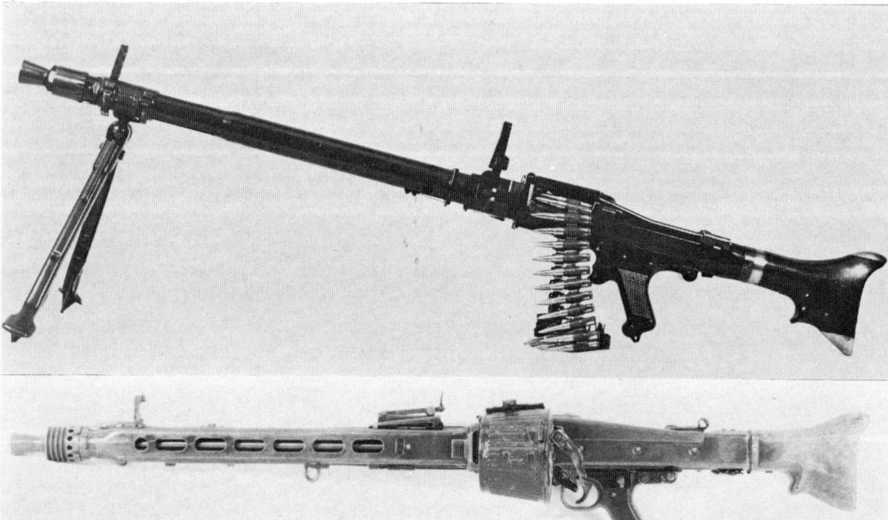

TOP LEFT: The basic infantry MG34 model. With its butt and bipod removed this gun was fitted into AFV mountings.

MIDDLE LEFT: The MG34 modified, with armoured barrel jacket. This gun is set up for ground use. The bipod-front sight assembly and buttstock were carried inside the vehicle for dismounted use.

BOTTOM LEFT: MG42 fitted with a 50 round belt-box, which could be fitted to this gun and the MG34, though not on AFV mountings inside the vehicle. The MG42 fired fully automatic only and was not adapted for AFV internal mountings.

TOP RIGHT: Panzer III crewman with the co-axial MG34 m. poised for dismounted action in a 'posed' photograph. The hull gun is a standard MG34.

BOTTOM RIGHT: Pzkpfw IV crewman cleaning weapons. The man in the reed-green suit is cleaning an MG34 m, whilst the other man attends to a P38 self-loading pistol.

4
124

Tank Crew's Personal Arms

ABOVE: Tank crewman with a Pistole 08 Luger.

TOP LEFT: Pistole 08 or 'Luger' was issued to tank crew as a side arm until supplies of the P38 became available to replace it. The Luger was still in service at the war's end.

MIDDLE LEFT: Pistole 38. This Walther design was intended to replace the Luger. It was a more rugged sidearm than the Luger and was issued to tank crews as a personal weapon.

TOP RIGHT: MP38. This particular example has a later safety MP40 bolt handle and magazine.

MIDDLE RIGHT: MP40 which replaced the MP38. It was constructed from stampings.

OPPOSITE BOTTOM LEFT: MP38 in service.

OPPOSITE BOTTOM RIGHT: MP38 armed tankmen examine an abandoned Russian T26.

BELOW: Mauser Karbiner 98K. This was the standard German infantry rifle during World War Two.

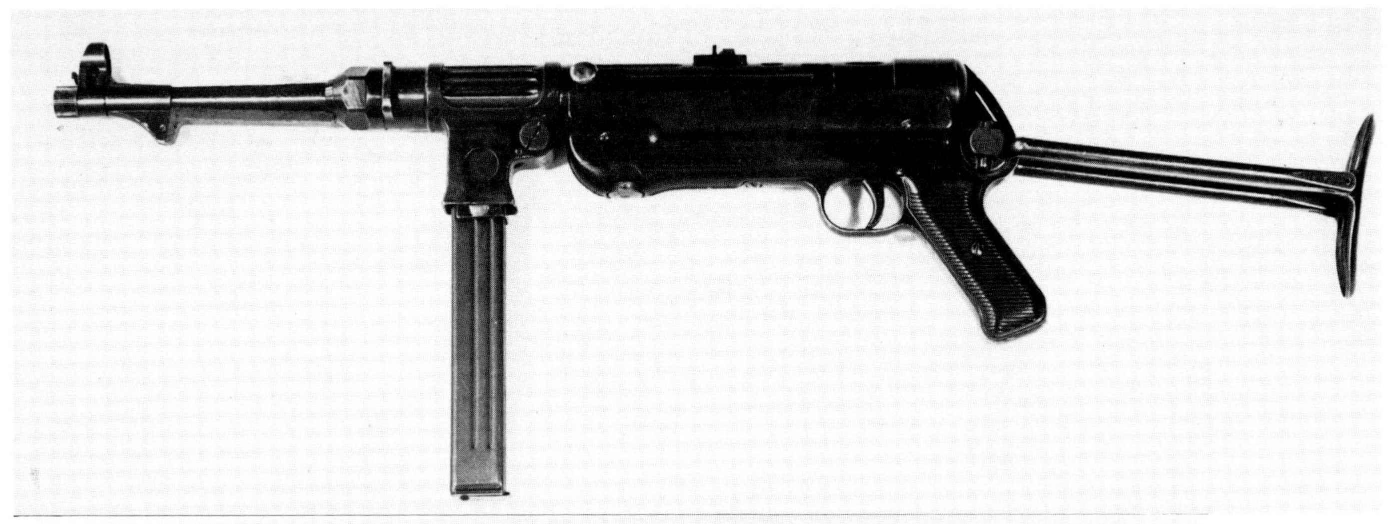

Support *(Versorgungs)* and Maintenance Companies

LEFT: Light repair shop of a regimental maintenance company, shows medium cars under repair. The Adler light truck nearest the camera has the 'G', synonymous with vehicles in General Guderians Panzergruppe.

BELOW: A mixed transport column of the wehrmacht. Horse-drawn and motorised. The Saloon-bodied cars with civil number plates and WH (Wehrmacht Heeres) on their wings later gave way to the military-pattern cars such as the Stoewer 40, next in line in this photograph, and pictured on the opposite page.

In addition to its fighting units, each tank regiment had a maintenance salvage company attached directly to Regimental HQ while each *Abteilung* had its own support company. In the early part of the war each *Abteilung* also had a 60-*tonne* capacity supply column attached but these were later amalgamated under Divisional Services for the sake of economy.

Regimental maintenance company: This was intended to provide first line servicing for all the regiment's equipment (i.e. breakdowns which it was judged would take less than 48 hours to repair) and to provide at least some means of recovering temporarily knocked out vehicles. Its composition and vehicle strength varied depending on the current regimental organisation and tank type but in general it comprised:

Company HQ: A small command group, 11 or 12 strong with one or two light command cars, a signals vehicle and a couple of dispatch riders.

Tank maintenance platoon for each *Abteilung.* This typically had a strength of between 50 and 60 personnel and was equipped mainly with workshop trucks (Kfz 51 and 79), maintenance vehicles (Kfz 61 or 69) and light repair vehicles (Kfz 2/40). Exact types varied depending on availability but typically they were based on the medium lorry chassis or the equivalent *Schell programm 3 tonne chassis* with specialist bodywork. At least one vehicle was likely to be a 5 *tonne* (or heavier) half-track fitted with demountable sheer-legs to facilitate engine changing. Established vehicle strength of such a platoon in 1944 was 14 lorries or cars and one motor-cycle, and this is likely to have been fairly constant for the whole war.

Tank salvage platoon. Specifically intended for recovering and bringing in broken down vehicles this platoon was about 45 strong and in 1944 had a complement of 15 vehicles and one dispatch rider motor-cycle. As the only sub-unit likely to come into direct contact with the enemy it was provided with limited small arms for local defence (LMG and SMG) and its vehicles included heavy recovery equipment. Initially these were normally 12 *tonne* or 18 *tonne* half-tracked lorries equipped for lifting and towing but with the advent of the *Pzkpfw V* and *VI* they were not sufficient. Special *Bergepanzer* (recovery) versions of the *Pzkpfw III, V* and *VI* were then substituted where appropriate. Since the platoon had to be able to function off roads its equipment was, at least theoretically, composed almost entirely of half-tracked or four-wheel drive vehicles.

Smaller sections were allocated to servicing the regiment's guns (Ordnance); to repairing and maintaining signals equipment; and to carrying a stock of spare parts. Each had four or five specialised vehicles and a personnel strength of between 15 and 25. There was also a small supply group – it could not really be called a column since its load capacity was only about 20 *tonnes* – which had a light car, seven or eight lorries and a motorcycle. Normal equipment would be 3 tonners or equivalent, though in Russia *Maultier* half-tracked lorries were often used.

Tank Abteilung support companies. Each *Abteilung* had its own support company, composition varying as the tank type and strength varied. No exact establishments are available but in general it would contain:

(a) HQ, a command unit about 20 strong with the usual two light cars or *Kettenkräder* and two lorries – one almost certainly a signals vehicle – plus one or two dispatch riders.

ABOVE: Sdkfz 2 Stoewer 40 light car of the wehrmacht. This type of body-work was standardised to fit on the commercial light car chassis' that were available.

BELOW: An Opel Blitz being freed from the mud by the combined efforts of army tankmen and SS personnel. The Opel Blitz medium truck saw extensive service on all fronts and was perhaps, the most popular and easily recognised vehicle in German army service.

(b) A small medical section commanded by an officer doctor and comprising two or three vehicles – sometimes including an armoured ambulance based on the *Sdkfz 251*.

(c) Strong maintenance, fuel and munition supply sections totalling perhaps 220 men with a big allocation of stores-carrying vehicles. 77 vehicles was the nominal establishment for a 1944-type Division.

(d) An administrative section to take care of the paperwork.

These support companies were fully motorised but were normally equipped with wheeled vehicles rather than half-tracks. The exceptions were usually in the maintenance sections which would have an allocation of 1 or 5-*tonne* half-track vehicles equipped for engineering work and, under difficult conditions, forward supply sections which might have *Maultiers* or even the proper *Schwerer Wehrmacht Schlepper (SWS* or heavy army tractor a half-tracked lorry of 5 *tonne* capacity).

Panzer Uniforms

ABOVE: Panther hull machine gunner/radio operator in green fatigue jacket.

Tanks crews' black uniform. When the *Panzer* arm was first formed it was decided to give armoured vehicle crews a distinctive uniform that was simultaneously practical and that recalled the old elite light cavalry from which they were supposed to derive. The result was a two-piece black suit, worn over a mouse-grey shirt and black tie. The suit jacket was short, double-breasted and had an open collar with fairly wide lapels; the left one could be folded over for warmth if required, two small buttons being provided on the right side of the chest to secure the lapel edge. Shoulder straps were provided as normal, though they were at times sewn down all round to avoid catching on projections, and the jacket had a fly front with concealed buttons. The accompanying trousers were long and full-cut, fastening above laced, black ankle boots. Original head-gear was the so-called *Panzer* beret, effectively a combination-type headgear in which a rather baggy beret cover concealed a stiff felted 'crash' liner to give some protection when riding in the vehicle. This was replaced from 1940-on by a black version of the normal *feldmütze* or forage cap which was in service until the war's end. It was supplemented, but never entirely replaced, by a black version of the *einheitsmütze,* the peaked forage cap which was introduced in 1943. Troops were also issued with the standard grey steel helmets.

These notes apply only to the special uniforms worn by Panzer unit personnel either manning or maintaining armoured vehicles. Supporting troops wore the normal Army uniform and equipment.

RIGHT: Crewman in the black uniform. Note he is wearing a 'polo-neck' jumper under his jacket. The lanyard ring into his jacket is probably attached to the butt of a P38 pistol carried inside the double-breasted jacket when the leather holster was not used. The object in his mouth is a very thick sandwich!

TOP LEFT: NSU built Kettenkraftrad in Russia.

FAR LEFT: A Phänomen ambulance of the Luftwaffe evacuating wounded by aircraft. The aircraft, a FW 189, operated closely with the panzer regiments as an aerial observation post.

LEFT: A Sdkfz 6 Praga 5 tonne recovery half-track passing a Sdkfz 250 of a panzer regiment.

Tank crews reed-green uniform. A two-piece green uniform identical in cut to the black one but made of denim was also issued to *Panzer* units. It was intended for summer wear but was in practice worn at any time and on occasions was even used as an over-jacket. There is no doubt that, being tough and easily washable, it was preferred to the black uniform in dirty conditions even though the latter was intended to hide stains. Some versions had a large patch pocket on the left breast.

Insignia. *Waffenfarbe* (arm of service colour) for *Panzer* troops was rose pink and this was worn on all uniforms as piping on the shoulder straps. Initially the collars and collar patches of the black uniform were also piped but the practice was discontinued for new stock in 1942. Rank insignia were confined to the shoulder straps, collar patches being a distinctive silver death's head *(Totenkopf)* design on a black or green background as appropriate. The 'normal' blue-green blacking was not, in principle, used on *Panzer* uniforms. The national emblem was worn in the appropriate place. So far as is known, support troops wore normal uniform with the appropriate *waffenfarber* piping. In this context it may be worth noting that all ranks in *24 Panzer Divison* wore golden-yellow piping, not pink, as a token of their cavalry origin.

On these two pages are a variety of tank crew uniforms ranging from the black suit and reed-green denims to the reversible winter suit. The pre-war uniform of the Oberleutnant below is interesting, being devoid of Nazi insignia. Compare this with the colour plate on page 17.

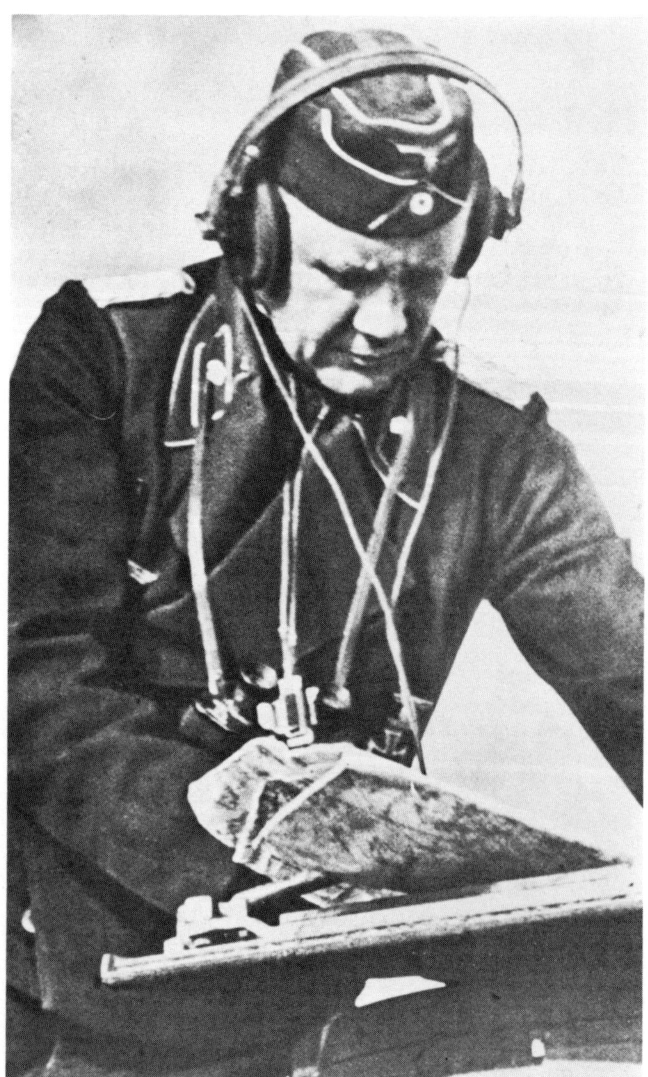

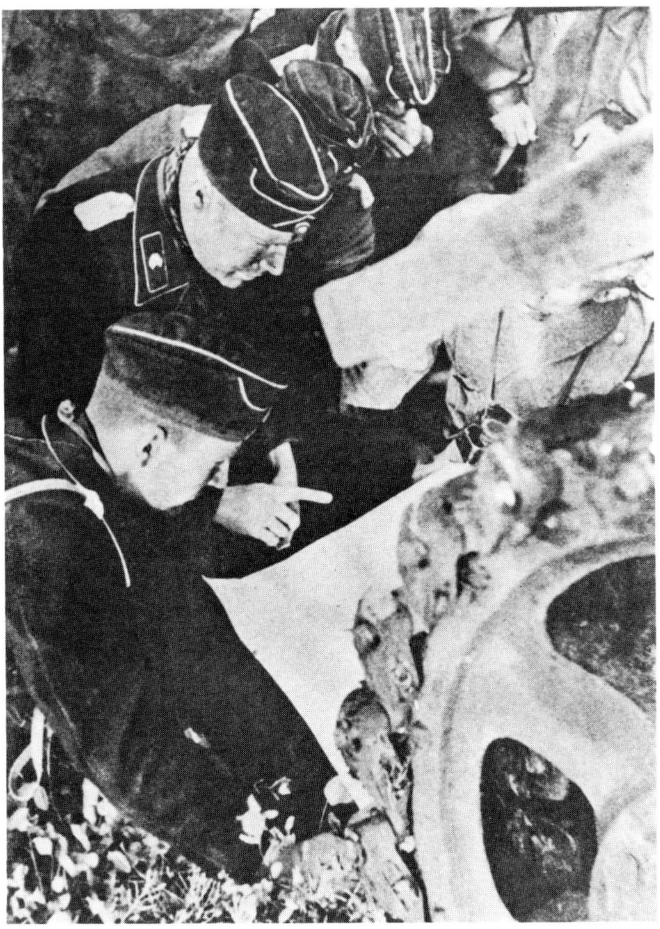

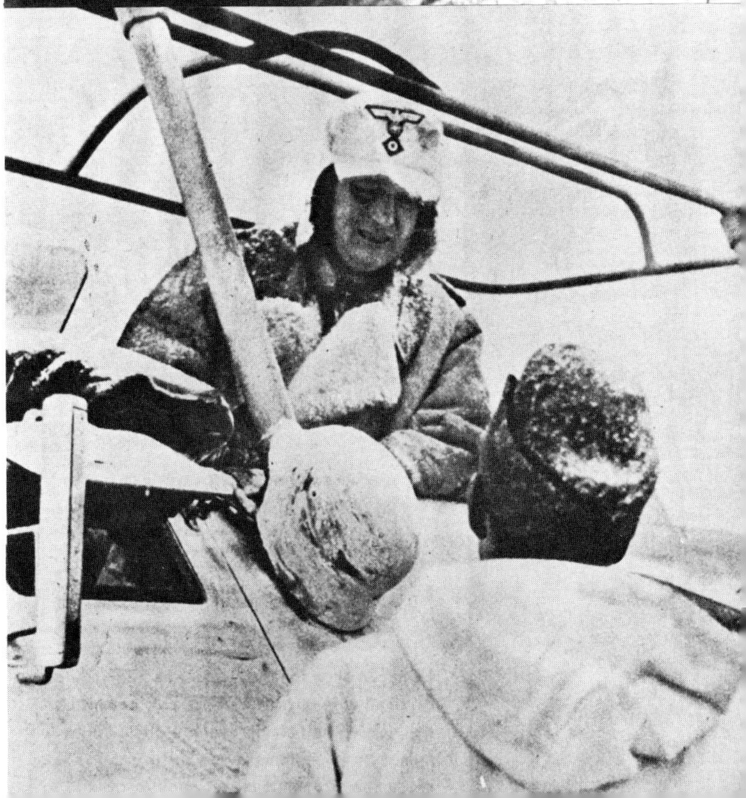

NOTIONAL ESTABLISHMENT FOR PZ UNITS 4/1944

REGTL. UNITS	PERSONNEL			LIGHT WEAPONS				VEHICLES				
	OFFICERS	NCOs	ORs	RIFLES	LMGs	SMGs	PISTOLS	TANKS	SP GUNS	M/T	M/CYCLES	
REGT. HQ.	4	3	7	9	-	2	3			2	2	
REGT. HQ. Coy.	5	54	56	37	16*	9	76	8	-	15	5	HQ Tanks or Crew included here
SP 3.7cm AA Pln.	1	27	49	19	8	16	42	-	3	7	2	(lower establishment)
MAINT/SUPPLY Coy.	6	39	185	209	17	4	4	-	-	68	6	
STANDARD (Pzkpfw IV) **ABTEILUNG**												
ABT. HQ.	4	3	7	10	1	1	3	-	-	2/3	2	
ABT.HQ. COY.	4	37	104	61	27*	24	61	8	3	19	8	HQ Tanks or Crew included here
SUPPORT COY.	7	51	123	137	3	21	20	-	-	66	2	
1 TANK COY.	4	50	39	6	34*	18	69	17	-	2	2	
2 TANK COY.	4	50	39	6	34*	18	69	17	-	2	2	
3 TANK COY.	4	50	39	6	34*	18	69	17	-	2	2	
4 TANK COY.	4	50	39	6	34*	18	69	17	-	2	2	

*These appear to include tank machine-guns.

An interesting pre-war parade photograph of a panzer scout company of a panzer reconnaissance battalion with Mercedes cars and early model Sdkfz 261's, and 221's and 263 armoured cars. Note the dress uniform of the soldier in the right foreground. The Sdkfz 261's have their aerials folded. Note also the battalion pennant on the lead car.

Tank Regiment Allocations to Army Divisions 1944

DIVISION	1	2	3	4	5	6	7	8	9	10	11	12	13
TANK REGT.	1	3	6	35	31	11	25	10	33	7	15	29	4

DIVISION	14	15	16	17	18	19	20	21	22	23	24	25	26
TANK REGT.	36	**	2	39	18	27	21	5	204	201	24	9	26

NOTE. 27 Pz Div. was short lived.
116 Pz Div. allocation was not clear.
SS Div. tank regts. called by name of their division.
GD and Panzer Lehr called by name of their division.
** at this time a Pz Grenadier Division.

ABOVE: Luftwaffe personnel man a 2 cm Flak 38 guarding a bridge, along with the Pzkpfw II Ausf B to the right.

Pzkpfw VI Ausf. E late model 'Tiger'

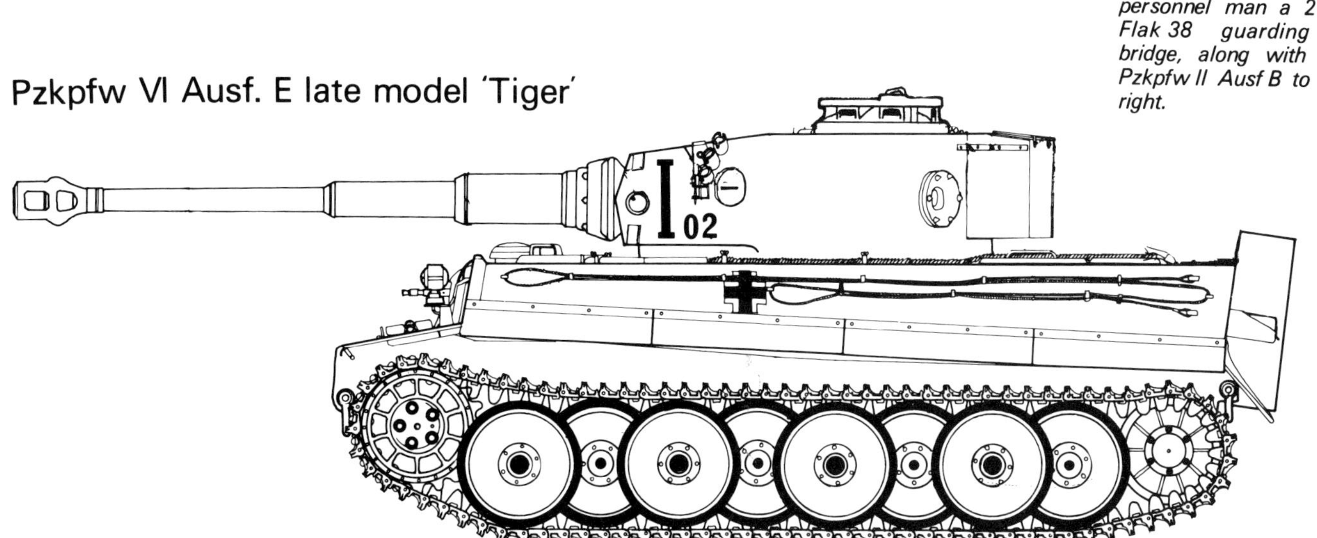

7.92 mm machine gun belts being loaded into a Pzkpfw III. These 100 round belts for the co-axial and bow MG34's were loaded into canvas bags when stowed inside the vehicle.

Colour Plates Page 17

(a) Tropical uniform as worn by troops in North Africa. The example shown is just one of the many variants. The tropical uniform was issued in two basic colours, green or tan, which 'washed out' to the neutral fabric. A simplified field cap (feldmütze) was usually decorated with the tropical type national insignia, blue-grey woven motif's on a red-brown backing which also appeared on the jacket. Dark green backing to tropical insignia was not unknown. The special canvas lace-up boots (which were often modified by troops) are shown here. The shorts are long trousers cut-down and sewn to the length shown. The weapon is the MP40 which along with pistols formed the main personal armament of tank crews in all theatres.

(b) The original black double-breasted panzer uniform as worn by an Oberleutnant issued to the embryo German Panzer Regiments. No Nazi national insignia was worn initially, the Nazi eagles being added during 1935. The 'Sam Browne' type cross-belt was later discarded from the officer's uniform, as later all ranks discarded the floppy beret concealing a crash helmet (worn for protection inside the AFV's) giving way to the headgear worn by figure 'f'.

(c) The winter reversible suit that was issued for service in Russia is shown here, white side outwards. The inner was either camouflaged (shown on figure 'e') or 'mouse-grey' as shown on the reverse of this example. The green armband was an identification worn to eliminate confusion between similar-clad Soviet troops, and the colours were changed daily for security purposes. This crewman has a captured Soviet PPSh 41 sub-machine gun; used by German troops whenever possible. They admired its 71 round magazine. The mittens worn here were designed to leave the index finger free for weapon firing etc.

Colour Plates Page 36

(d) A young Leutnant of Panzer Regiment Herman Göring. This Luftwaffe division wore the army panzer uniform with Luftwaffe insignia, cuff title and white waffenfarb. Numerous variations existed on the basic theme, such as white backing to the collar totenkopfs. The ribbon in the collar button-hole is that of the Iron Cross. The medal is worn (under the wearers hand) along with the Luftwaffe ground combat badge. (Erdkampfabzeichen der Luftwaffe).

(e) The winter reversible suit worn camouflage-side outwards by a Hauptman (Captain) who's rank is shown in green on a black patch on the upper left arm. This captain wears the officers cap (schirmütze) with pink waffenfarb piping. These caps were usually modified for field wear by removing the grommet and silver cap cords.

(f) The reed-green panzer suit, cut along similar lines to the double-breasted black version. A large pocket was provided – stitched on a slant – over the left side of the body. This suit was intended for summer wear but was often worn over the black suit in service. Normal insignia was sewn onto this suit and decorations pinned on as normal. The wearer is an Unteroffizier. Green fatigues cut to the army pattern were also worn by tank crewmen as seen on page 49.